THE CARE OF TOMORROW'S ELDERLY

THE CARE OF TOMORROW'S ELDERLY

MARION EIN LEWIN
&
SEAN SULLIVAN

American Enterprise Institute for Public Policy Research
Washington, D.C.

Distributed by arrangement with

UPA, Inc.
4720 Boston Way   3 Henrietta Street
Lanham, Md. 20706   London WC2E 8LU England

Library of Congress Cataloging-in-Publication Data

The care of tomorrow's elderly.

(AEI studies ; 487)
Includes index.
1. Aged—Care—United States. 2. Retirement
income—United States. 3. Aged—Government
policy—United States. I. Lewin, Marion
Ein. II. Sullivan, Sean. III. Series.
HV1461.C37 1989   362.6'0973   88-35120
ISBN 0-8447-3680-5 (alk. paper)

1 3 5 7 9 10 8 6 4 2

AEI Studies 487

Printed in the United States of America

Contents

LIST OF TABLES

Acknowledgments

We thank the Commonwealth Fund for its support of the research and the symposium that made this book possible. We also want to express our thanks to the following people who offered helpful critiques of its content at various points along the way: Steve Thomas at the Commonwealth Fund, Lynn Lewis, and Marion C. Strong.

MARION EIN LEWIN
SEAN SULLIVAN

Contributors

Marvin H. Kosters
Director of Economic Policy Studies
American Enterprise Institute

Marion Ein Lewin
Senior Staff Officer, Institute of Medicine,
National Academy of Sciences
(former Director of Health Policy Studies, AEI)

John H. Makin
Resident Scholar and Director of Fiscal Policy Studies
American Enterprise Institute

Jack A. Meyer
President, New Directions for Policy
(former Director of Health Policy Studies, AEI)

Marilyn Moon
Director, Public Policy Institute
American Association of Retired Persons

Michael Novak
George F. Jewett Scholar in Religion, Philosophy, and Public Policy
American Enterprise Institute

Allen Schick
Professor of Public Policy
University of Maryland

Timothy M. Smeeding
Director, Institute for Public Policy Studies and
Professor of Economics, Vanderbilt University

Sean Sullivan
Vice President, New Directions for Policy
(former Senior Policy Analyst, AEI)

Susan Vroman
Associate Professor of Economics
Georgetown University

Wayne Vroman
Senior Research Associate
The Urban Institute

Stanley Wallack
President, Life Plans, Inc., and
Director, Bigel Institute for Health, Brandeis University

John C. Weicher
Associate Director, Office of Management and Budget
(on leave from AEI, where he holds the F. K. Weyerhaeuser Chair in
Public Policy Research)

1
Overview

Marion Ein Lewin and Sean Sullivan

The chapters in this volume were written against the backdrop of an ongoing national debate between those urging new federal entitlements to long-term care for older Americans and those seeking to enhance the role of the private market. Many of these authors are AEI scholars approaching the subject from the perspectives of disciplines other than the economics of health care, enabling them to offer a wider range of analyses and recommendations. In general, they argue for a continued mixture of public and private financing and organizational arrangements. But they urge a change in the mixture, toward greater reliance in the future on private resources and the market to meet the long-term needs of the elderly. Several of them, moreover, argue for rethinking some of the basic premises behind public policies concerning the elderly.

Many of the articles point toward a redefined role for the federal government with respect to the needs of older Americans for health care and adequate income in retirement. This role, in brief, is to assume responsibility for the poorest while encouraging private market responses to take care of the preponderance of citizens sixty-five years old or more. The changing realities of demographic trends and fiscal constraints—and the improved economic status of most of the elderly—argue *not* for an additional federal entitlement program but for targeting public aid to the most vulnerable, while encouraging the market to offer affordable protection against catastrophic expenditures such as nursing home stays or extended home care services to the great majority.

The United States must develop a coherent longer-term strategy for meeting the health care and retirement needs of its elderly and a more consistent set of policies flowing from this strategy. The policy agenda should be responsive to the changed requirements and circumstances of older Americans—needs for greater protection against the potentially ruinous expenses of long-term care, taking into account their increased wealth and higher incomes relative to the rest of the population. These policies must be fair and humane in their application to the diversity of situations in which the elderly find

1

themselves. They cannot, however, be based on the status of the aged that lay behind the creation of Medicare two decades ago. They must be fundamentally—not just incrementally—reshaped.

Appropriate Roles for Government and the Market

Although government can identify particular problems and help with their solutions, it cannot and should not try to solve them alone. The appropriate roles of public and private sectors should be carefully defined and weighed to avoid assigning ill-considered responsibilities to either.

Assumptions that lay behind policies made twenty years ago have to be reexamined and those policies redesigned to reflect current economic and social realities. Medicare was established when many of America's elderly citizens had no or inadequate health insurance and could not afford to purchase such protection. The program was established to pay for acute medical care expenses but not comprehensive coverage of long-term and chronic care. As the government works to reshape Medicare to respond more effectively to the broad-based health care requirements of older Americans, the need to target limited public dollars better is imperative, especially in view of other domestic and international priorities.

As several of the authors in this volume make clear, the economic situation of older Americans has changed dramatically for the better over the past two decades. The elderly now have relatively fewer poor among their ranks than the general population. Only 12.4 percent of Americans sixty-five and older are living below the poverty line today, in contrast to 13.7 percent of the total population; twenty years ago, the respective percentages were 28.5 and 13.3. Elderly poverty has been reduced by more than half, while the overall poverty rate has remained essentially unchanged.

The major improvement in both the absolute and the relative economic status of the elderly over the past two decades stands in sharp contrast to the ominous increase in poverty among children. Since 1973, the poverty rate for those under eighteen has risen more than 50 percent, with one of five children now living in poverty. This situation is especially troubling because of the evidence that poor children tend to become poor adults.

Older Americans are highly differentiated in their tastes, their circumstances, and their preferences. A large and growing number can afford some measure of private protection against the potentially ruinous expenses of long-term care, as a greater choice of insurance products is being offered on the private market. (Marion Ein Lewin and Stanley Wallack discuss this in their chapter.) The burgeoning private insurance market, which is better equipped than government to respond flexibly to their varying choices, can reasonably be expected to meet the needs of a substantial number of the elderly by the end of the century.

Government can play a role in stimulating private market forces through leveraging—for example, by offering to "backstop" private insurers with stop-loss protection above a certain limit. Demonstrations are under way in several states to guarantee eventual Medicaid protection against the catastrophic expenses of long-term care to people who purchase private policies when their coverage runs out, without the requirement of spending down to poverty levels. This combined public-private approach should stimulate demand for private insurance. While the market has its limitations in providing access to health care, it should be given the opportunity and the encouragement to go as far as it can toward meeting the needs of older Americans for protection against long-term-care outlays before government steps forward to take up the burden.

The private market, however, cannot solve the problem of providing long-term care to elderly who lack the purchasing power to participate in such a market. The proper role of government here is to help provide this purchasing power to those who otherwise lack the means to make effective choices in the marketplace. The private sector can provide avenues through which this purchasing power can be used to create more effective choices to satisfy consumer desires.

This approach would leave to government more responsibility for the shrinking proportion of older Americans who qualify as "poor." Through restructured Medicare and Medicaid programs, the federal and state governments should cast their safety nets wider to take in elderly who are not now considered poor enough for assistance and must, therefore, truly impoverish themselves before qualifying for Medicaid.

Policy Trade-offs

We face a difficult challenge in trying to meet pent-up demands for services—for child care, education, and health benefits—out of a depleted federal Treasury. Massive budget deficits will continue to drive our social policy for the foreseeable future, and that means tight constraints on any new spending. These dynamics are creating a tension between the needs of young families and the calls for additional services for older citizens.

Americans sixty-five and older at present make up 11 percent of

3

the population, but 29 percent of all federal outlays and 48 percent of domestic spending are accounted for by Medicare and social security. Although prospective payment for inpatient hospital stays and other efforts to control costs have slowed their rise a little, Medicare expenditures are still expected to grow faster than the gross national product (GNP) over the next twenty years. Yet we need to make much greater investments in tomorrow's workers, who will have to finance this growth and keep social security benefits flowing to increasing numbers of elderly as well. This can only be done if the aging of the population is at least matched by increases in the productivity of the labor force.

The profound social and demographic changes taking place pose significant challenges to the American standard of living in the decades ahead. To remain competitive in the integrated world economy—a basic condition for increasing real incomes—will require large investments in both our human and our physical capital. This means increased spending on education, training, and R&D, as well as on basic social programs like health care for poor children, to make the next generation more productive.

The United States is not alone in facing these policy dilemmas concerning its older citizens. All the industrial democracies are confronted by the same challenges of aging populations and slower economic growth, challenges that are much more serious for some other nations, such as Japan and West Germany. By the year 2025, when 38 percent of Americans will be over sixty-five, the corresponding proportion in several other developed countries will be 50 percent or more.

The modern social welfare states are all caught in the same trap. In designing social policies that have entitled most of their older citizens to fairly generous pension and health benefits (more generous in most European countries than in the United States), they have placed an inexorably increasing burden of financing these benefits on their working populations. As the ineluctable arithmetic of demography continues to operate, an ever-growing proportion of retirees must be supported by the payroll taxes of a shrinking share of active workers.

This brings us to another theme of this volume: the need to restructure public policies to ensure that we maintain an acceptable degree of equity between the generations. To do so will require that we find a way to challenge the universal expectation of increasing entitlements for all middle-class Americans as they leave the work force. This expectation is a seemingly unassailable barrier to all political efforts at making basic changes in social security or Medicare.

4

Yet these are the kinds of changes that will have to be made if we are to avoid an eventual choice between unacceptable tax levels and bankrupt programs.

Basic changes are required to diminish the traditional proclivity merely to apply band-aids to problems, such as, for example, raising the retirement age again, as was done in the last round of reforms that supposedly "fixed" the social security problem for good. Jack Meyer discusses some of these more fundamental reforms in his chapter on fitting retirement policy to shifting demographic and economic conditions.

The Policy Agenda

In formulating fresh policy approaches to these problems, we must not feel limited to options that are on the present agenda or to established ways of thinking. The current environment for policy making—with wider recognition of the challenges facing us, as well as increasing pressure *and* ability to respond flexibly to changing economic and social conditions—makes fundamental reforms in our policies more feasible. Such reforms should be based on these convictions:

• Policies must acknowledge the need to enhance our country's productive capacity, not only to improve our competitive standing but also to create the economic basis for more secure retirement.
• People want improved benefits, but they do not want programs that are wasteful or attempt to meet needs that are not legitimate.
• Responsibility for meeting legitimate needs must be shared in a prudent way between the public and the private sectors, since we cannot continue living beyond our national means.

Our nation must rethink the terms of many of its social welfare programs, now outdated by demographic trends and new economic realities. The former terms are no longer sustainable and threaten to cause bitter divisions within our body politic. They must be restated to make clearer what our citizens have a right to expect from government and what they must do for themselves.

A crucial part of restructuring our social policy arrangements will involve carving a larger role for private saving and insurance in meeting the future needs of older Americans. Private pensions and other forms of saving, plus private health insurance against the costs of long-term care, must become a larger part of the future mixture of public and private means for ensuring the security of the elderly in our society.

5

We should reverse incentives now built into social security and private pension plans that encourage people to choose early retirement over continued work. Benefits from public programs will have to be related more to recipients' incomes, so that the better-off elderly are not subsidized to the same extent as those with much lower incomes. And tax incentives should be used to broaden the coverage of the private pension system and Supplemental Security Income (SSI) guarantees raised to help the elderly who are still poor.

This is not the time for a big expansion of federal programs, especially in their present form, with so many perverse features and disincentives built into them. But it may be the time to restore a better balance between public and private responsibilities and resources.

Summaries of the Chapters

In "Wealth and Poverty among the Elderly," John Weicher provides a necessary starting point for considering the needs of the elderly by examining their economic status. Analyzing original data, he finds that a substantial redistribution of wealth from the young to the elderly took place between 1977 and 1983, with the "young" old aged sixty-five to seventy-four enjoying the greatest gain. The largest increases in older Americans' wealth came from their financial assets, but home equity remains the principal form of wealth for the majority. Elder Americans have also been gaining in income in comparison with younger households, largely because of the indexing of social security benefits. Weicher notes, however, that low-income elderly renters have not fared so well and remain relatively poor, although they are declining as a proportion of the total population. And he observes that the considerable wealth tied up in the home equity of older citizens remains, for now, just a potential source of liquidity for funding long-term-care insurance or other needs, given the failure to date of reverse annuity mortgages to gain much acceptance in the marketplace.

In "Health Policy: Spending More and Protecting Less," Allen Schick offers an economic and political context to help explain some of the vexing anomalies of our current health care system. Schick believes that economic factors do not suffice to explain the marked variances in health care spending between the United States and other industrialized nations. The dominating role of medical providers in shaping health care policy has been a contributing factor. Most of all, however, he sees the dilemma of high expenditures and limited protection resulting from political processes and values unique to America: the grafting of equity objectives onto an entrepre-

6

neurial medical system, our government's traditional reluctance to interfere with the medical enterprise, the avoidance of explicitly redistributive policies, and reliance on incrementalism and decrementalism rather than fundamental reforms to bring about change.

John Makin's chapter, "Economic Growth and the Health Care Budget," begins with a macroeconomic perspective on the doubling of health care expenditures as a share of GNP in the past twenty years. Makin observes that the greatest share of growing public spending for health care goes for the elderly and that demographic trends raise a serious question of intergenerational equity in the United States—whether it is fair, as well as financially feasible, to make a shrinking working population finance health care for an expanding population of retirees through higher Medicare payroll taxes. Slower-than-expected economic growth has combined with the aging of the population to put the future viability of current financing arrangements in question. Makin also asks whether, in the long run, we might be better off in both economic and health terms by spending more on the young and the poor.

Marvin Kosters proposes an innovative approach to policies concerning the elderly, based on considering real outlays rather than merely public expenditures. With respect to those older Americans who want to keep working, Kosters argues for changing the tax treatment of social security benefits—lowering marginal rates to encourage more recipients to earn additional income that can be used to meet health care and other needs. With respect to financing long-term care in particular, he suggests that we might optimize both economic and human outcomes by giving individuals direct cash payments with which they can obtain a full range of health and social services, both formally and informally. The payments would be based on determinations of the nature and extent of illness or impairment. While acknowledging the difficulty of developing such a classification system, Kosters notes that precedents exist in the workers' compensation system and in private disability schemes. His proposal would seek to establish consumer sovereignty over the purchase of long-term-care services by paying individuals instead of institutions and would permit payment to informal care givers for some services now provided voluntarily.

Wayne and Susan Vroman, in their chapter "The Increase in Early Retirement since 1969," present some startling findings on the extent to which older male workers are choosing to leave the work force before they reach sixty-five. During the three decades from 1954 to 1984, the labor force participation of males aged fifty-five to sixty-four dropped twenty percentage points, from 89 to 69 percent. The

Vromans conclude that most of these men are not retiring early principally for reasons of health but because of generous financial incentives and changed social attitudes toward early retirement. They doubt that recent legislative changes in social security—gradually raising the age of eligibility for full retirement benefits, taxing a portion of the benefits of higher-income recipients, and providing a delayed retirement credit for those who work past age sixty-five—will prove sufficient to stem the rising tide of early retirements. Nor do the authors believe that liberalizing the earnings test for social security recipients will call forth much extra work effort from those who have already retired. If we want to reverse the trend toward early retirement, the Vromans suggest that we may have to go so far as fully taxing social security benefits, offsetting them by the amount of other pension benefits, and raising the age at which workers become eligible to receive early retirement benefits in the first place. Even then, they are not sure how much effect such actions will have in a society in which early retirement has become an important goal for many citizens.

Jack Meyer has contributed two chapters to this volume. In "Reforming Medicare and Medicaid," he proposes restructuring Medicare and Medicaid to fill better some of the critical unmet needs of the elderly and to create a more complementary relationship between these public programs and the kinds of private sector initiatives discussed in other chapters. Specifically, Meyer advocates less first-dollar coverage and more protection against large back-end costs under Medicare (a concept that has just been embodied in the new catastrophic care health bill) and outlines a stop-loss benefit plan for both acute and long-term care, which the new bill does not provide. Such a Medicare enhancement, combined with some private insurance coverage of long-term-care expenses, could significantly reduce the number of moderate and low-income elderly who find themselves forced to "spend down" their resources to become eligible for Medicaid when confronting the prospect of catastrophic outlays for nursing home care. Savings to Medicaid brought about by this type of reform could be used to make that program more equitable by improving the scope of coverage for the poor elderly population.

In his chapter "Matching Policies for Retirement Years with Changing Demographic and Economic Conditions," Meyer examines the "mismatch" between public and private policies toward retirement and the actual conditions of our older citizens. These policies encourage Americans to retire early, when they are living longer and remaining healthier; they also impose an increasing financial burden on a working population that is declining relative to the growing

8

number of retirees. At the same time, our policies ignore the different economic situations of the elderly, paying out social security benefits, for example, as if all older Americans were in equal need. And these policies favor the "young old," who are much better able to take care of themselves than the "old old."

Meyer argues that such policies are out of line with demographic trends and economic realities. He recommends changes that would encourage longer working lives and recycle a portion of current benefits from the better-off elderly to those who are not so well off, for example, by taxing social security benefits just as we do private pension benefits. Meyer also argues more broadly for policies that would increase productivity, private saving, and economic growth, such as capitalizing on the experience and skills of older workers instead of letting them leave the labor force prematurely. Such changes would enable companies to provide greater private pension benefits to more of their retired workers, making them less dependent on social security.

In their chapter, "Can the Elderly Afford Long-Term Care?" Marilyn Moon and Timothy Smeeding review the data on the improving economic status of the elderly to show that an increasing number of older Americans will be able to shoulder the costs of long-term care. Even many with modest incomes may be able to purchase private insurance to cover those expenses, as such protection becomes more available and is purchased at earlier ages. But a significant in-between group of lower-to-middle-income elderly will remain who cannot afford such coverage in the foreseeable future but who do not want to be pauperized to qualify for Medicaid. Moon and Smeeding examine the potential for private insurance by focusing on its likely costs as a portion of older Americans' future incomes. They also offer policy options for subsidizing the lower-to-middle-income group that falls between the market for private insurance and eligibility for Medicaid.

Expanding on the theme of private market response to these needs, Marion Ein Lewin and Stanley Wallack, in "Strategies for Financing Long-Term Care," predict that private sector risk-sharing models currently being developed to finance long-term care stand a good chance of being successful and affordable. Often-voiced pessimistic appraisals of their potential to meet the funding challenges of tomorrow's elderly have been based on the limited track record of first-generation nursing home indemnity products. The capacity for private financing of long-term care is greater than once thought, and, in varying degrees, such programs are potentially affordable for many Americans.

9

Lewin and Wallack contend that insurance products are beginning to respond more effectively to market demand and, specifically, to the awareness that the elderly have different perceptions of risk and a strong desire to maintain their independence and their life style. Many of the more recent approaches and options seek to integrate the provision of acute and long-term-care services in a managed care setting or, in the case of life care communities, to combine health, housing, and continuing care. Lewin and Wallack believe that creative private-public partnerships to finance long-term care represent our best hope for meeting the challenge of providing for the needs of an aging population humanely and effectively in an era of limited resources.

Michael Novak rounds off the volume in a philosophical vein. He begins by noting the great improvement that today's elderly enjoy in the total circumstances of their lives, compared with their parents or grandparents. While acknowledging our society's success in bringing this about, Novak observes that there are still enough older Americans whose needs are not being met to cause us and our public policy makers great concern. He points out that Americans, unlike citizens of other developed countries, have preferred meritocratic to egalitarian social philosophies, causing them to shun such ideas as national health insurance while defending their social security benefits as something they have earned. But Novak argues that health is not by nature as much a matter of merit as are most other social goods and may be a candidate for a different kind of public policy toward those who cannot afford protection. He suggests that, in the larger balance of things, the well-off elderly may have to think about forgoing some of their "entitled" benefits in favor of not-so-well-off older citizens and children alike.

The chapters in this volume present a varied set of analyses and policy options for meeting the long-term needs of present and future older Americans. They point away from massive new reliance on public programs or government guarantees, both because the resources are not there and because the varied needs of a diverse and more affluent elderly population can better be met in other ways. Public programs can be expanded modestly, but, more important, they can be restructured to target help to those who really need it. At the same time, the private market can be expanded greatly to help a growing majority of individuals meet their own needs for long-term health care—and to give them more attractive choices for doing so.

2
Wealth and Poverty among the Elderly
John C. Weicher

The economic well-being of the elderly has been improving at the same time that public policy has become increasingly concerned with the rising costs of providing health care to them. Both the wealth and the income of the elderly have increased, relative to the rest of the population, as well as absolutely. This paper focuses on the increasing wealth of the elderly and its implications for health policy. In most discussions of general well-being, wealth has received less attention than income. Home equity, however, has been regarded as a possible source of additional income for general living expenses as well as for health care.

Two recent surveys provide new information about the wealth of the elderly. These are (1) the Federal Reserve Board (FRB) surveys of consumer asset holdings in 1977 and 1983: the Survey of Consumer Credit (SCC) and the Survey of Consumer Finances (SCF), respectively, and (2) a special supplement to the Bureau of the Census Survey of Income and Program Participation (SIPP), on a quarterly basis beginning in 1984.

The surveys have different strengths and weaknesses. SIPP has much the larger sample, but far fewer questions about asset holdings. Indeed, its basic purpose is to obtain information about low-income benefit programs. The SCC and SCF are themselves not fully consistent; the latter has more detailed information about income and the value of assets.[1] Reporting error is a particularly serious problem in household surveys of assets; both surveys had difficulties measuring household equity in unincorporated businesses. Both surveys are limited to the civilian, noninstitutional population and do not include nursing home residents; the elderly that are included are those who might need long-term health care in the future. This paper relies primarily on the FRB surveys, since they cover a longer period and have received more analytical attention.

The Increasingly Wealthy Elderly

Between 1977 and 1983 there was a substantial redistribution of wealth from the young to the elderly. Table 2–1 shows mean wealth by age. Households with the head under age fifty-five lost, in real terms; households with the head over fifty-five gained. Except for the oldest group, there is a monotonically increasing relationship between age of household head and gain in wealth. The largest increases were enjoyed by the "young elderly," age sixty-five to seventy-four; the largest decline was suffered by the youngest age group, with head of household under twenty-five. The youngest category of the elderly became the richest group, on average, displacing the group immediately below them in the age distribution. The elderly as a whole enjoyed a larger average gain than any group below them, although the fifty-five to sixty-four age group gained almost as much. The elderly moved from being the third richest to the second richest group on average, passing the forty-five to fifty-four age group. Real mean wealth per elderly household rose from about $81,000 to about $111,000. The share of total household wealth owned by elderly households increased from 25 to 31 percent in just six years.[2]

The SIPP data show a similar pattern. The major difference is that the elderly had on average less wealth than the two immediately younger groups in 1984. Their share of total household wealth was about 28 percent. A year later, their share rose to 30 percent. The elderly reported the largest mean increase of any group, in both absolute and percentage terms, but they remained less wealthy than the fifty-five to sixty-four age group.[3]

The difference between the FRB survey in 1983 and the SIPP survey in 1984 may reflect changes in asset values; the stock market was rising and interest rates were falling. It is more likely, however, to be explained by the differences between the surveys. The point here is not to make minute comparisons between them, but to note that both show elderly households having on average a considerable and an increasing net worth. The best available evidence from other sources, moreover, also indicates that the wealth of the elderly has been growing relative to younger households. The Annual Housing Survey and the Current Population Survey report that both house values and homeownership rates increased more for the elderly than for other households between 1977 and 1983.

Wealth holdings are highly skewed, and wealth is much more concentrated than income. Mean values are therefore less useful than medians in conveying information about the well-being of the typical household. Unfortunately, relatively little information about median

TABLE 2-1
MEAN NET WORTH OF HOUSEHOLD HEAD, 1977–1985
(1985 dollars)

Age of Household Head, 1977 and 1983

	Under 25	25–29	30–34	35–44	45–54	55–64	65–69	70–74	75 and over	All elderly	All
1977	11,500	21,400	42,400	74,100	100,600	104,600	97,200	79,100	71,600	81,300	68,700
1983	7,300	18,400	36,800	68,500	98,900	140,000	150,800	137,300	82,100	110,800	79,200
Percentage change	−37	−14	−13	−8	−2	+34	+55	+74	+15	+36	+15

Age of Household Head, 1984 and 1985

	Under 35	35–44	45–54	55–64	65 and over	All
1984	23,400	71,000	118,600	137,000	108,300	81,400
1985	22,300	76,100	101,500	134,300	116,800	81,300
Percentage change	−4	+7	−14	−2	+8	0

NOTE: Percentage changes are calculated from unrounded figures and may differ from changes as calculated from the figures in the table.

SOURCES: The top panel, unpublished tabulations from the 1977 *Survey of Consumer Credit* and 1983 *Survey of Consumer Finances;* and John C. Weicher and Susan M. Wachter, "The Distribution of Wealth among Families: Increasing Inequality?" table 4; the bottom panel, John M. McNeil and Enrique J. Lamas, "Year-Apart Estimates of Household Net Worth from the Survey of Income and Program Participation," table 1.

13

wealth, or other positional measures of the distribution, is readily available. The three most recent surveys report medians for various age categories, but not consistently. The two SIPP surveys report a median wealth for elderly households of about $60,000 in 1985 dollars, with a decline from 1984 to 1985. The 1983 SCF reported lower medians for each of two age categories among the elderly, about $55,000 for the young elderly and over $40,000 for those seventy-five and over.[4] These are still substantial amounts.

Table 2–2 shows the changes in value for financial assets and home equity held by the elderly between 1977 and 1983. These are the two largest categories of wealth. Financial assets increased relative to home equity for all three age groups, although only slightly more for the oldest households. The young elderly did better in every category—and rather spectacularly better in financial assets.

These changes have some interesting implications concerning the financial acumen and well-being of the elderly. To understand these implications, it is useful to recollect the changes in the economy between 1977 and 1983. It was not a typical period, but comprised two distinct and unusual subperiods. The first three years, 1977 to 1980, witnessed extremely high inflation by American peacetime standards. At the end of 1979, monetary policy changed abruptly. During the second half of the period, the annual inflation rate was reduced from almost 10 percent to less than 4 percent.

In these subperiods, relative asset values changed dramatically. From 1977 to 1980, as inflation crested, the nominal value of the typical owner-occupied home rose by 45 percent, common stocks rose by 21 percent, and corporate and municipal bonds each fell by about 30 percent.[5] During the disinflation of 1980 to 1983, home values rose by 14 percent, common stocks by 15 percent, and corporate bonds by 1 percent. Municipal bonds, however, fell another 10 percent. In real terms, houses became more valuable between 1977 and 1980, while stocks and bonds lost value. Stocks then improved between 1980 and 1983 (strictly speaking, from 1982 to 1983), while houses and bonds lost value. Over the whole period, houses and stocks both appreciated slightly in real terms, while the decline in the value of bonds was horrendous.

Changes in values of other real assets paralleled the changes in home values, but were even more exaggerated. Philatelists and collectors of objets d'art enjoyed extraordinary real capital gains during the 1970s. An index of U.S. postage stamps, for example, tripled in real terms between 1977 and 1981, then dropped by over 15 percent through 1983. Farm land values increased by 17 percent in real terms

TABLE 2-2
MEAN WEALTH OF ELDERLY HOUSEHOLDS BY TYPE OF ASSET, 1977 AND 1983
(1985 dollars)

Asset Category	Household Head Age 65–69		Household Head Age 70–74		Household Head Age 75 and Over	
	1977	1983	1977	1983	1977	1983
Financial assets	32,700	60,200	32,300	69,300	33,200	35,100
Home equity	53,900	57,900	36,300	47,100	36,400	34,000

SOURCE: Weicher and Wachter, "The Distribution of Wealth among Families," and unpublished tabulations from the 1977 *Survey of Consumer Credit* and the 1983 *Survey of Consumer Finances.*

TABLE 2-3
PROJECTED AND ACTUAL WEALTH OF HOMEOWNERS WHO WERE OVER
SIXTY-FIVE IN 1977, 1980, AND 1983
(1985 dollars)

Year	Total Wealth	Financial Assets	Home Equity
1977 (Actual)	93,200	36,600	56,800
1980 (Projected)	95,900	30,300	65,600
1983 (Projected)	90,800	28,000	62,900
1983 (Actual)	107,200	52,900	54,300

NOTE: Projections assume that household asset holdings were unchanged after 1977, and values for asset holdings changed in accord with price indexes for each category. Actual wealth is reported wealth holdings in 1977 and 1983.
SOURCE: William B. Shear and John C. Weicher, "Disinflation and the Value of Homeowners' Wealth: Who Benefits?" Paper presented at the annual meeting of the American Economic Association, New York, December 1985 (revised).

from 1977 to 1980, then dropped back almost to their 1977 level by 1983. Both continued to fall in nominal terms through 1987; in real terms, they are still losing value in 1988.

These were dramatic and unusual changes. Any elderly American living in the late 1970s had experienced only one comparable period, the years immediately after World War II. Prices rose by about 10 percent annually from 1945 to 1948 after removal of wartime price controls, but then the inflation rate quickly abated to about 2½ percent annually through 1951 and continued to decline during the 1950s. The immediate postwar inflation, however, had an obvious proximate cause—the removal of wartime price controls—and was widely regarded at the time as an aberration. The inflationary spurt of the late 1970s came after a decade of gradually accelerating inflation, in an environment where the costs and difficulty of controlling inflation were generally thought to be too high, politically if not economically.

Compared with other age groups, the elderly hold a disproportionately large share of financial assets, particularly common stocks and most particularly bonds. It would therefore be reasonable to expect that they suffered more than other age groups from economic changes between 1977 and 1983. This did not happen, however. Table 2-3 attempts to describe wealth changes of elderly homeowners in 1977 over the next six years. It compares the actual change in wealth, as nearly as it can be estimated, with the change that would have been expected if elderly homeowners had simply kept the same portfolio of assets over the entire period.[6]

Had they been passive investors, elderly homeowners would have gained slightly between 1977 and 1980. They would have lost slightly more between 1980 and 1983, winding up 1.5 percent poorer in real terms over the whole period. Their financial assets would have lost over 20 percent; their homes would have appreciated by about 10 percent.

The reality was very different. Elderly homeowners enjoyed a 15 percent overall gain, composed of almost a 50 percent increase in the value of financial assets—in the face of declining markets—and a minimal increase in home values. The latter may perhaps be explained as a normal part of the household aging process. Death of one spouse may lead the other to move into a smaller house or a condominium, while still remaining a homeowner. A possible explanation for the stellar performance of elderly investors is that, as retirees, they can devote more time and attention to analyzing changes in financial markets. This is more important for them than for younger households whose income is derived almost entirely from labor.

The SIPP data, as well as the general movements in asset prices, make it likely that the elderly have continued to improve their position since 1983. Stocks and bonds have both increased in value. Even after the stock market crashed in October 1987, their prices are higher than they were in 1983. Moreover, the homeownership rate among the elderly is continuing to rise, as table 2–4 shows. This contrasts with the rest of the population. Homeownership among younger households has declined through the 1980s, although it may now be stabilizing at about its 1970 level.

Increased homeownership among the elderly probably reflects the cumulative effect of decisions by individual households to continue owning their homes, rather than decisions of elderly renters to purchase homes. A trivial number of elderly renters choose to become homeowners; the Annual Housing Survey reports no more than 3,000 in any year since 1973. At least twice as many owners become renters. But over the past decade more elderly owners have continued to own when they move, and more have chosen to remain in their homes for a longer time. That is, elderly households have found continuing homeownership desirable, for either financial or personal reasons. The rising ownership rate is certainly a manifestation of increasing economic well-being, better health, or both. The elderly can afford to keep their homes longer and are better able to maintain them.

17

TABLE 2-4
HOMEOWNERSHIP AMONG THE ELDERLY, 1974–1987
(percent)

| | Age of Household Head | | | |
Year	65–69	70–74	75 and over	All households
1974	73.1	69.7	66.8	64.6
1975	73.6	69.4	67.3	64.7
1976	73.6	71.5	67.2	64.8
1977	74.0	71.1	67.2	64.8
1978	74.7	71.3	67.9	65.2
1979	75.8	72.5	67.4	65.5
1980	77.3	72.7	67.8	65.6
1981	77.5	75.2	70.0	65.3
1982	77.8	75.1	70.9	64.7
1983	78.6	75.3	71.9	64.7
1984	79.1	75.4	71.4	64.4
1985	79.3	76.7	69.7	63.9
1986	79.0	76.7	69.3	63.8
1987	79.1	77.2	70.2	64.0

SOURCE: U.S. Department of Housing and Urban Development, unpublished tables.

Continuing Problems of the Poor Elderly

Although the typical elderly household is much wealthier than it used to be, many old people still have financial problems. The 1984 SIPP results show almost 20 percent of elderly households with net worth less than $10,000 (in 1984 dollars; about $10,400 in 1985 dollars).

Tables 2–5 through 2–7 provide some further information on the relatively poor elderly. For several categories of elderly households, they show mean 1977 and 1983 wealth based on income and age of the household head. The income brackets may conveniently be termed "low," "moderate," and "middle," respectively. Higher-income households are omitted from the tables because there were few high-income elderly households in the 1977 SCC.

There are clear differences by income and by age. Middle-income households in all age groups enjoyed substantial gains in real wealth. Higher-income households are omitted from the tables because there were few of them in the 1977 SCC, but it seems likely that they experienced real gains, in all age groups. The real mean net worth

TABLE 2-5
MEAN WEALTH OF THE ELDERLY BY INCOME, 1977 AND 1983
(1985 dollars)

Income	Wealth[a]	
	1977	1983
Household Head Age 65–69		
Under 8,500	26,400	30,500
8,500–17,000	64,000	61,500
17,000–34,000	109,000	153,700
Household Head Age 70–74		
Under 8,500	28,300	28,800
8,500–17,000	72,300	79,100
17,000–34,000	130,200	146,600
Household Head Age 75 and Over		
Under 8,500	36,300	22,500
8,500–17,000	73,200	71,300
17,000–34,000	129,300	151,800

NOTE: Samples for income classes above $34,000 are too small to report reliable means for 1977.
a. Unlike tables 2–6 and 2–7, the wealth figures in this table include "other property," such as unincorporated businesses and farms, which few households own.
SOURCE: Unpublished tabulations from the 1977 *Survey of Consumer Credit* and the 1983 *Survey of Consumer Finances*.

for all high-income elderly households increased from about $275,000 in 1975 to $310,000 in 1983. Low- and moderate-income households with heads under seventy-five, however, generally gained much less, and low-income households with heads over seventy-five suffered substantial real losses. A similar pattern appears in the SIPP data for 1984 and 1985. Higher-income elderly households generally gained, while lower-income elderly households suffered losses.[7]

Table 2–6 shows mean financial asset holdings. Low-income elderly households had limited financial assets in 1977 and suffered losses over the period. Moderate-income households had more assets but also mainly incurred losses. Middle-income households had fairly substantial holdings and roughly held their own. Since the elderly as a whole enjoyed a large increase in mean financial assets (see table 2–2), the gains clearly were concentrated among the high-income households.

Financial asset holdings and changes were about the same for

19

TABLE 2-6
MEAN FINANCIAL ASSETS OF THE ELDERLY BY INCOME, 1977 AND 1983
(1985 dollars)

Income	Financial Assets	
	1977	1983
Household Head Age 65–69		
Under 8,500	5,500	4,800
8,500–17,000	13,300	14,300
17,000–34,000	44,800	48,100
Household Head Age 70–74		
Under 8,500	5,000	3,100
8,500–17,000	29,100	20,600
17,000–34,000	51,900	57,300
Household Head Age 75 and Over		
Under 8,500	9,600	4,500
8,500–17,000	32,300	26,100
17,000–34,000	73,700	68,600

NOTE: Samples for income classes above $34,000 are too small to report reliable means for 1977.
SOURCE: Unpublished tabulations from the 1977 *Survey of Consumer Credit* and the 1983 *Survey of Consumer Finances.*

both owners and renters in each age and income category, so table 2–6 can reasonably represent each group as well as the elderly as a whole. Table 2–7 presents the changes in home equity for homeowners. The difference between home equity and financial assets is striking. Home equity increased substantially for nearly every group; all at least held their own.

It is clear from the three tables that homeowners and renters had different experiences between 1977 and 1983, and that homeownership was the main factor contributing to gains in wealth or mitigating losses. Because financial assets constitute nearly all the wealth of renters, table 2–6 is a close approximation of their mean net worth. Table 2–7 essentially shows the difference in wealth between owners and renters. (The most important form of wealth omitted in these tables is "other property," such as unincorporated businesses and farms, which few households own. This category is included in table 2–5.) Except for the poorest and oldest group, each category of homeowner enjoyed a substantial increase in mean wealth. Low-income renters were less fortunate.

One group of low- and moderate-income homeowners has prob-

TABLE 2-7

MEAN HOME EQUITY OF ELDERLY HOMEOWNERS BY INCOME,
1977 AND 1983
(1985 dollars)

Income	Home Equity	
	1977	1983
Household Head Age 65–69		
Under 8,500	18,600	31,800
8,500–17,000	41,500	43,200
17,000–34,000	55,100	82,900
Household Head Age 70–74		
Under 8,500	22,900	33,600
8,500–17,000	40,100	57,200
17,000–34,000	45,100	76,500
Household Head Age 75 and Over		
Under 8,500	25,400	29,900
8,500–17,000	40,700	52,200
17,000–34,000	49,200	61,900

NOTE: Samples for income classes above $34,000 are too small to report reliable means for 1977.
SOURCE: Unpublished tabulations from the 1977 *Survey of Consumer Credit* and the 1983 *Survey of Consumer Finances*.

ably fared no better than renters. Mobile home owners are unlikely to have much home equity or enjoy much appreciation in the value of their homes. Because many rent their homesites, they have not benefited from increases in land values either.

The tables paint an overly bleak picture of the elderly poor, however. Real incomes and homeownership rates both rose between 1977 and 1983. The proportion of low-income renters among the elderly declined from 18 to 15 percent, and the proportion of moderate-income renters from 8 to 7 percent. The proportion owning mobile homes also fell, from 5 to 4 percent.

As a first approximation, then, the fraction of elderly households without much wealth to rely on fell from 31 to 26 percent between 1977 and 1983—a declining majority, but surely still a significant one.

The implications of these findings for health care are straightforward. Low-income elderly renters, and probably mobile home owners as well, have faced a problem of meeting unexpected medical (or other) expenses. In all likelihood, the problem has been getting worse.

21

TABLE 2–8
MEDIAN REAL INCOME OF THE ELDERLY AND OTHER HOUSEHOLDS,
1973–1987
(1985 dollars)

	Elderly			Non-elderly	All
Year	Families[a]	Individuals	Households[a]	Households	Households
1973	14,500	6,200	9,700	27,100	23,800
1977	15,400	6,500	10,700	26,400	22,900
1980	16,700	6,600	11,400	26,900	22,900
1983	18,200	7,500	12,600	25,600	21,600
1985	19,200	7,600	13,300	27,000	23,600
1987	19,700	7,766	13,568	28,371	24,597

NOTE: Real incomes calculated using the experimental CPI-U-XI for years before 1983, rather than the official CPI.
a. A family is defined as two or more related individuals living together; a household is defined as whoever lives in a housing unit, including families, single people living alone, and unrelated individuals living together.
SOURCE: U.S. Bureau of the Census, Series P-60, *Consumer Income*, various years.

Income and Poverty

It is illuminating to compare recent changes in wealth with the corresponding changes in income for the elderly. Table 2–8 shows the trends in median income of the elderly and other households since 1973, including the 1977–1983 period for which wealth data are also available. Real incomes for the elderly have been rising steadily, albeit more slowly than real net worth. Between 1977 and 1983, the median real income for all elderly households and for elderly families rose by about 18 percent. The median for elderly individuals living alone rose by 15 percent. Overall, the proportion of elderly in the low- and moderate-income groups declined from 71 to 61 percent.[8] The record in this period is part of a longer trend. The income of the elderly has been rising steadily since long before 1973, although table 2–8 goes back only to that year.

The table also shows that the elderly have been gaining in income (as well as wealth) relative to younger households. The experience since 1973 has been dramatically different among the generations. The year 1973 is often cited as the beginning of a period of stagnation in the U.S. economy. Some measures of economic well-being still

TABLE 2-9
POVERTY RATE OF THE ELDERLY, 1967–1987
(percent)

	Poverty Rate	
Year	Official	Corrected
1967	29.7	29.7
1973	16.3	15.8
1979	15.2	12.9
1980	15.7	12.8
1981	15.3	12.3
1982	14.6	11.5
1983	13.8	11.0
1984	12.4	9.5
1985	12.6	9.5
1986	12.4	9.9
1987	12.2	9.9

SOURCE: Daniel H. Weinberg, "Implications of Mismeasuring the Consumer Price Index for Poverty Statistics," ISP Technical Analysis Paper No. 34, March 1987, U.S. Department of Health and Human Services.

show 1973 as the peak year. Table 2–8 shows that the real income of nonelderly households was no greater in 1985 than it had been twelve years earlier.[9] Only in the most recent years of this unusually long economic expansion has the median income of nonelderly households finally exceeded its 1973 level.

One factor contributing to the income pattern for nonelderly households was the severe double recession of 1980 to 1982. It is particularly remarkable that real income for the elderly continued to rise at about the same rate during these years, while real income for nonelderly households fell about 5 percent. This is undoubtedly due in part to the indexation of social security benefits; inflation in the first two recessionary years remained high.

The incidence of poverty among the elderly has also been steadily declining. Since at least 1967, their poverty rate has fallen every year except 1984, through each of three recessions as well as through the years of economic growth. This is shown in the right-hand column of table 2–9, where the incidence of poverty is computed using the GNP deflator rather than the official consumer price index (CPI) to measure inflation.[10]

Wealth, Health, and Policy

Few of the elderly are millionaires, but most are wealthy—and becoming even wealthier—at least compared with younger households. The majority appear able to afford comprehensive long-term-care insurance on the private market. A minority, however, clearly have limited resources. They would undoubtedly have trouble coping unaided with major medical problems not covered by Medicare or other insurance. This minority consists largely of relatively low-income renters. Middle- and upper-income renters have substantial financial assets, and even low-income homeowners have substantial home equity, although by and large they do not have much else.

Except for the small group of upper- and middle-income renters, the wealth of the elderly is predominantly in their homes. Two-thirds of the elderly own their own homes and do not live in mobile homes. Some 8 million elderly households had homes worth at least $30,000 in 1983, according to the Annual Housing Survey; few were encumbered with a mortgage.

The magnitude of this illiquid wealth raises some public policy issues. The possibility of monetizing it to pay for living expenses or long-term health care costs has been discussed for more than a decade. The most popular approach, in the literature at least, has been the reverse annuity mortgage (RAM). But the literature on RAMs is schizophrenic. On the one hand, there is a litany of problems for both lender and homeowner, centering on the risk that the homeowner will be forced to move at an advanced age. On the other hand, analysts are intrigued by all that equity in all those homes sitting there untapped. The average values for home equity are many times the cost of private long-term-care insurance policies, for example. A recent survey reports premiums of up to $1,500 for a sixty-five-year-old and $4,500 for a seventy-five-year-old. The mean home equity figures are all large enough to cover those premiums for at least ten years for the low-income sixty-five-year-old homeowner and for at least five years for the low-income seventy-five-year-old owner. They would cover the middle-income homeowner up to age eighty-five, in both cases. But if the owner were still alive by then, he or she could well lose both the house and the insurance.

The problems have proved insoluble so far, and few RAMs have been written. To encourage RAMs, some analysts and policy makers favor federal programs like FHA insurance, or a secondary market. A pilot insurance program was part of the 1987 housing act; preliminary regulations for the program have been developed by HUD, and the pilot program is expected to be operating by the spring of 1989.

24

I do not think the disappointing record of RAMs indicates a public policy failure, however. RAMs have simply been rejected in the marketplace. There have been extraordinary innovations in the mortgage market over the past fifteen years. The most important is the adjustable-rate mortgage (ARM), developed without FHA insurance or Federal National Mortgage Association (FNMA) purchases, indeed without government sanction and in spite of congressional opposition. ARMs were offered first by state-chartered savings and loan associations and commercial banks. Only after ARMs had proved their viability did Congress permit federally chartered institutions to offer them.

The market reaction to RAMs is not unique. A number of alternative mortgage instruments were proposed in the 1970s and found wanting. RAMs have appealed to some financial economists, and on paper they could "work," but they have frightened consumers. The pilot program in the housing act is unlikely to change consumers' minds.

The continuing policy interest in RAMs reflects a genuine concern, however. The elderly are getting richer, in terms of both income and wealth, at the same time that their health benefits have been growing. Indeed, it is likely that the elderly are getting richer in part *because* of the benefits. The availability of Medicare and private health insurance probably has dramatically reduced the need for the elderly to sell their homes or liquidate other assets. While this assertion is likely to remain a conjecture for lack of empirical information, it is surely plausible. If it is true, then public policy to maintain the health of the elderly has indirectly promoted a redistribution of wealth from the young to the old—by allowing the elderly to keep their assets longer.

Policies to facilitate the use of those assets to meet further costs of health care would thus seem especially appropriate. The nature of the policies, however, is far from clear. If RAMs are not the answer—and so far they are not—it seems fair to say that the public policy analysts do not know what is. But some answer should be found. It is probably unfair to tax the working population to provide long-term care for the elderly when most of the elderly are wealthier than most of the workers. Even if it is fair, it is politically questionable.

Notes

1. For a comparison of the surveys, see Richard T. Curtin, F. Thomas Juster, and James N. Morgan, "Survey of Estimates of Wealth: An Assessment of Quality" (Paper presented at the Conference on Research on Income and Wealth, Baltimore, Md., March 1987).

2. As an aside, it is worth noting that table 2–1 and all succeeding tables compare the same age groups over time. Obviously these are not the same households. The only basis for identifying any group of households over time is to compare the sixty-five to sixty-nine year-old group in 1977 with the seventy to seventy-four year-old group in 1983. In table 2–1, and in most succeeding tables, the differences between the sixty-five to sixty-nine and seventy to seventy-four age groups in 1983 are small, so that the sixty-five to sixty-nine comparisons over time can be read as a reasonable approximation of the change in wealth for the sixty-five to sixty-nine age group of 1977. The exceptions occur for "moderate-income" households in tables 2–5 through 2–7.

3. The data on other property in the 1983 SCF are probably more complete than the data for 1977. For this reason, the increases shown in the top panel of table 2–1 may be overstated. I have also calculated net worth as the sum of financial assets and home equity; the age profiles and changes from 1977 to 1983 are similar, except that the oldest group shows no gain rather than a 15 percent increase.

4. The 1983 SCF data appear in table 7 in Robert B. Avery, Gregory E. Elliehausen, Glenn B. Canner, and Thomas A. Gustafson, "Survey of Consumer Finances, 1983: A Second Report," *Federal Reserve Bulletin* 70 (December 1984), pp. 857–68. The 1984 SIPP data are in table 4, U.S. Bureau of the Census, *Household Wealth and Asset Ownership: 1984*, Current Population Reports, Series P-70, no. 7 (July 1986). The 1985 data are from table 1, John M. McNeil and Enrique J. Lamas, "Year-Apart Estimates of Household Net Worth from the Survey of Income and Program Participation" (Paper presented at the Conference on Research on Income and Wealth, Baltimore, Md., March 1987). The first two report medians for the seventy-five-and-over age group; they differ by $16,000.

5. Throughout this paper inflation is measured by the GNP deflator. Home values are measured by the Census Bureau's Price Index of New One-Family Homes Sold, the broadest index; common stocks by Standard and Poor's 500-stock index; corporate bonds by Standard and Poor's AAA corporate bond index; and municipal bonds by Standard and Poor's municipal bond index.

6. These calculations assume that each household's 1977 holdings are the same as the base for the index used to measure changes; the indexes are the same ones referred to in note 4. The two Fed surveys included different households; the 1983 sample is limited to homeowning households with the head at least seventy-one years old, to be comparable to the 1977 data.

7. See McNeil and Lamas, "Year-Apart Estimates of Household Net Worth," table 3. They report mean net worth by quintile for several household types among the elderly, but not for the elderly as a whole. Female-headed elderly households (most of them single persons) in all income brackets gained; lower-income married couples suffered losses; lower-income males had no change.

8. For this reason, the distribution of wealth for the elderly as a whole does not indicate an increase in the number of poor. Between 1977 and 1983 the distribution of wealth among the elderly became noticeably more une-

qual. The coefficient of variation, a common statistical measure of dispersion, increased from about .14 to .19 for both age groups shown in table 2–1. This occurred because of an increasing difference between the richer and the poorer elderly, rather than because of growth in the numbers who were poor. Both the rich and the poor gained, but the rich gained more.

9. This does not mean that 1973 was the best year for the typical non-elderly household. Median real income in 1979, not shown in the table, was $27,600.

10. It is generally agreed that the CPI mismeasured the change in the cost of living during the inflation of 1965 to 1982. See John C. Weicher, "Mismeasuring Poverty and Progress," *Cato Journal* 6 (Winter 1987), pp. 715–30. Before 1983, the CPI measured the cost of homeownership in any given year as the cost of buying a home for the families who bought homes in that year, rather than as the cost of living in a home for all owners. The cost of buying a home was measured as the full purchase price and the total of all mortgage payments for fifteen years, in effect giving double weight to the purchase price. The CPI was changed in 1983; homeownership is now measured as the annual rental value of owner-occupied homes, as it has been by the GNP deflator. The corrected measure is used in table 2–9 for consistency over time as well as for a more accurate measure of the cost of living for elderly households, very few of whom buy homes in any year.

3
Health Policy: Spending More and Protecting Less

Allen Schick

The United States is spending more on health care than ever before, but many Americans are dissatisfied with what the money is buying. Health care expenditures reached $458 billion in 1985, three times the amount spent a decade earlier.[1] Almost 11 percent of the gross national product is now allocated to health, compared with less than 6 percent when Medicare and Medicaid were enacted in 1965. Increased spending has vastly improved access to medical care, modestly extended life expectancy, and somewhat relieved the financial strains of illness. It has also led to a great deal of complaining about the health care system. Physicians gripe about the paperwork and the controls, hospitals about cost pressures and frequent rules changes, and patients about inadequate coverage. Just about everyone complains about cutbacks; yet costs continue to soar.

The problem of rising costs during a period of cutbacks is one of several anomalies besetting health care in the United States.

• Despite more than $100 billion spent each year on Medicare and Medicaid, the elderly spend about the same percentage of their income on health services that they did before these programs were established. To make matters worse, the financial burden is inversely related to income. The poorer the elderly are, the larger the portion of their income spent on health care.[2]

• Despite freezes and other cost controls, medical inflation has not abated. Health care prices soared an estimated 7.7 percent in 1986, about seven times the general inflation rate. Despite Medicare's heralded shift from cost reimbursement to prospective payment, hospitals have widened their profit margins in recent years. Profits have been estimated at between 12–17 percent in some studies, much higher than before cost controls were imposed.[3]

• Despite the Medicare-Medicaid objective of protecting all aged and poor Americans, the number of unprotected persons is rising. More than 35 million people lack medical insurance during all or part

29

of the year. Fewer than half of those at or below the poverty level are covered by Medicaid.[4]
• Despite the fact that Medicare was designed for the elderly, it is Medicaid that finances most of their long-term care. One of every three Medicaid dollars goes to care for elderly people who are poor or who have "spent down" or concealed their assets. More than 40 percent is spent on long-term care, including care of the mentally retarded. In fact, Medicaid spends ten times more on each aged recipient than on each poor child receiving assistance.[5]

The picture that emerges from these anomalous conditions is of shrinking coverage in the face of escalating costs. The two sides of the problem are related because some reductions in coverage have resulted from efforts to curtail spiraling costs.

This chapter discusses these anomalies and their policy implications. It first looks at economic explanations, then at political ones.

The Inadequacy of Economic Explanations

One popular explanation of the cost side of the dilemma is that the federal government has generated enormous inefficiencies by paying for capacity and utilization decisions over which it has little or no control. According to this line of reasoning, because the government picks up so much of the tab, providers and beneficiaries have strong incentives to increase the supply and use of medical services. Pursuant to this diagnosis, the appropriate prescriptions would be to make beneficiaries and providers bear some or all of the added cost of their actions. Recipients should pay through cost-sharing requirements, providers through capitation schemes that limit payments per patient or case. These reforms, it has been argued, would reduce costs by restoring market incentives to the health sector.

Those who have urged adoption of these efficiency-inducing reforms acknowledge that the changes made in recent years have not yet produced the intended results. But they insist that it takes time to modify the behavior of those accustomed to governmental largesse. Moreover, they note, cost sharing is still rather limited. Medicare's supplementary medical insurance (SMI) deductible, frozen at $75 for many years, has declined from 70 percent of the cost of average per capita benefits in 1967 to less than 8 percent in 1987. Health maintenance organizations (HMOs) and other capitation schemes are the exception; fee-for-service arrangements still predominate for physician services. Finally, Medicare patients pay hardly anything from the second through the sixtieth day of hospitalization. More than

30

TABLE 3-1
HEALTH CARE EXPENDITURES PER CAPITA AND AS A PERCENTAGE OF
GROSS DOMESTIC PRODUCT IN SIX NATIONS, SELECTED YEARS,
1965–1986

	Per Capita (U.S.$)		Percentage of GDP			
	1982	1986	1965	1983	1986	Percent increase, 1965–1986
Canada	989	1,370	6.1	8.6	8.5	39
France	931	1,039	5.2	8.1	8.5	63
Germany	974	1,031	5.1	8.2	8.1	59
Sweden	1,168	1,195	5.6	9.1	9.1	62
United Kingdom	508	711	4.1	6.2	6.2	51
United States	1,388	1,926	6.0	10.8	11.1	85

SOURCE: "Data Watch," *Health Affairs* (Fall 1988), pp. 106, 107, 109.

three-quarters of these patients have "medigap" policies that pay most of the hospital charges not covered by Medicare.

The adequacy of these arguments is called into question by comparing U.S. health care with conditions in other countries. A comparison reveals that the United States does indeed buy relatively limited coverage at high cost. The cost-coverage anomaly is uniquely American.

Table 3–1 shows health care expenditures per capita and as a percentage of gross domestic product (GDP). The figures reveal that, while other industrialized democracies have also been compelled to devote an increasing share of national output to health care, the United States ranks highest in health spending as a proportion of GDP. It also outranks the other countries in per capita expenditures on medical care.[6] Sweden, which has a substantially different system of providing health care, is the only country that comes close to the United States in the per capita amount or percentage of GDP allocated to health care.

Whatever drives up health care costs in the United States, public spending does not appear to be a sufficient explanation. Table 3–2 compares, the public burden for financing or providing health care in the United States and six other countries. If public expenditure were primarily responsible for spiraling health care costs, one would expect the public sector to pay a higher portion of the total health care bill in the United States than in other countries. But the data in

31

TABLE 3-2
PUBLIC EXPENDITURE ON AND COVERAGE OF HEALTH CARE, 1983

	Public Expenditure on Health Care as a % of GDP	Public Expenditure on Health Care as a % of Total Health Expenditure	% of Population Eligible for Hospital Care under Public Scheme	Public Share of Hospital Care Outlays (%)
Canada	6.2	73	100	91
France	6.6	71	100	92
Germany	6.6[a]	80	75	79
Japan	5.0	75	100	89
Sweden	8.8	92	100	100
United Kingdom	5.5	89	100	99
United States	4.5	42	40	54

a. 1982 data.
SOURCE: OECD, *Measuring Health Care, 1960–1983*.

table 3–2 conclusively show the opposite. The United States allocates a higher share of GDP to health care than any other country. Yet its public sector spends a lower percentage of GDP on health than any of the other countries. Moreover, U.S. public spending constitutes the smallest portion of total health care expenditures. Only 42 percent of total health care spending is financed by public funds in the United States, compared with 70 percent or more in the other countries.

The relatively low level of public financial involvement is largely due to the low percentage of the population eligible for public financing (or provision) of hospital care and to the smaller public share of total hospital outlays. The United States is lowest on both of these measures. Though public assistance for hospitalization is universal in most of the other countries, only 40 percent of Americans have public coverage. And although the public share of hospital expenditures ranges between 70 percent and 100 percent elsewhere, it is only 54 percent in the United States.

One would expect relatively low public spending in the United States to have a dampening effect on total health expenditures. Instead, table 3–2 provides additional evidence of the high cost–low coverage anomaly that plagues American health care.

The case for cost sharing and other efficiency-inducing reforms rests on two assumptions. First, users demand and receive more free or low-priced services than they would pay for on their own. Second, providers supply more than the necessary volume of services. In view of the status of the United States as a high-expenditure country, one would expect it to have a high supply of, and demand for, medical services. Table 3–3 compares demographic, capacity, and utilization conditions in the United States and selected countries. By none of these measures are conditions in the United States so markedly different as to burden it with significantly higher health expenditures.

The first measures are the percentages of the population between the age of sixty-five and seventy-four and above the age of seventy-five. It is well documented that the elderly require more health services than younger people. Accordingly, as the populations of mature democracies have aged, their health care expenditures have increased. But although demographic trends help explain the pervasive rise in health care costs, they do not explain why the United States outspends other countries. The percentage of the population age sixty-five or older is significantly higher in France, Germany, Sweden, and the United Kingdom, all of which have lower per capita and relative health expenditures.

The second set of measures in table 3–3 pertains to the capacity

TABLE 3-3
DEMAND AND SUPPLY FACTORS ASSOCIATED WITH HEALTH CARE, 1982 AND 1983

	Demography		Capacity		Utilization	
	% of population age 65–74	% of population 75 or older	Hospital beds per 1,000 population (1982)	Physicians per 1,000 population (1982)	Inpatient days per capita (1982)	Physican contacts per capita (1983)
Canada	6.2	4.0	6.9	1.9	2.1	5.5[a]
France	7.1	6.1	6.9	2.1	3.1	4.7
Germany	8.8	6.2	11.1	2.4	3.4	n.a.
Japan	6.2	3.5	11.9	1.4	3.6	n.a.
Sweden	9.9	6.9	14.0	2.3	4.8[a]	2.7
United Kingdom	8.9	6.2	8.1	1.3	2.4[a]	4.2
United States	7.1	4.8	5.9	2.0	1.7[a]	4.6

a. 1981 figures.
n.a. = not available.
SOURCES: Population data from United Nations, Department of Economic and Social Affairs, *Demographic Yearbook*, 1984. Health data from OECD, *Measuring Health Care 1960–1983*.

TABLE 3–4

HOSPITAL AND PHYSICIAN UTILIZATION RATES,

1982 AND 1983

	Hospital Utilization		Physician Utilization
	Number of days average beds used, 1982	Utilization rate (percent)	Annual number of patient contacts per physician, 1983
Canada	305	84	2,860[a]
France	279	76	2,256
Germany	306	84	n.a.
Japan	302	83	n.a.
Sweden	341	93	1,153
United Kingdom	298	82	3,255
United States	287	79	2,291

n.a. = not available.
a. 1981 figure.
SOURCE: OECD, *Measuring Health Care 1960–1983*.

of the health care system. Capacity is conventionally measured in terms of the number of hospital beds and physicians per 1,000 population. The relationship between capacity and spending levels is often assumed to be different in health care than in other sectors of the economy. In a market economy, excess capacity is expected to generate lower prices. In the health sector, it may push prices upward as providers seek to recover the cost of acquiring the capacity by charging higher fees or by providing additional services. The data in table 3–3 suggest that the United States is not oversupplied compared with selected other countries. It ranks lowest in the supply of hospital beds and in the middle range in the availability of physicians.

The third set of measures deals with the utilization of health care services. The per capita numbers of inpatient days and of physician visits are standard utilization measures. One would expect to find a strong correlation between utilization rates and expenditure levels. But despite its high health care expenditures, the United States has the fewest inpatient days per capita, and it is only about average in per capita physician contacts.

The two previous sets of measures, capacity and utilization, interact in determining the efficiency of a health care system—that is, the extent to which available capacity is used. Table 3–4 estimates the number of days each hospital bed is used during the year and the annual number of patient visits per physician. The United States is

35

somewhat below other countries in the utilization of hospital capacity and in the middle range in utilization of physicians. The data suggest that the United States is moderately less efficient than some other countries. But the added cost of idle or underused capacity does not come close to accounting for this country's significantly higher medical expenditures.

It should be clear that economic factors do not adequately explain why the United States spends more than other countries on health care but buys less coverage. A number of factors not considered here undoubtedly contribute to differences among democratic countries. For example, the conditions affecting supply and consumption of medical services vary among countries. These include differences in nutritional practices, environmental quality, personal attitudes toward health, the social status of physicians, and the organization of hospitals. Anyone seeking to improve health care or to lower its cost must take these factors into account.

In comparison with other countries, health care in the United States is dominated by providers. Physicians and hospitals are extraordinarily influential in determining the type and cost of care provided to patients. Their influence is reflected in the specialization of health care, the rapid infusion of technology and other costly innovations, and the intensiveness of certain services. Compared with citizens of other countries, Americans are much more likely to be cared for by a specialized physician than by a general practitioner, to have access to the latest technology, and to be placed in intensive-care facilities. All these practices add significantly to the cost of health care.

The factors discussed thus far do not include differences in the political culture and behavior of democratic countries. Yet if one turns from the cost side of the problem to the coverage issue, it seems highly probable that political actions influence the distribution of health care. Alone among major democracies, the United States has made a political decision not to provide universal health care coverage, not to establish a comprehensive public health insurance scheme, not to finance long-term care for the elderly through Medicare, and not to regulate the supply of, or demand for, medical services heavily. These political decisions distinguish the United States from other democratic countries.

Table 3–5 compares salient features of the health care delivery and financing systems of five democratic countries. The data reinforce the conclusion that economic factors alone do not explain marked variances in health care expenditures. Health spending is markedly

TABLE 3–5

CHARACTERISTICS OF HEALTH CARE SYSTEMS IN SELECTED COUNTRIES

	West Germany	Canada	Sweden	United Kingdom	United States
Type of protection	Comprehensive public insurance	Comprehensive public insurance	National health service	National health service	Mixed public-private
Principal means of providing care	Private	Private	Public	Public	Private
Basic health care coverage	93% public insurance	99% public insurance	100% public insurance	100% public insurance	20% public, 65% private insurance
% lacking coverage	0	1	0	0	15
Cost sharing for covered services	Nominal	Nominal	Nominal	Nominal	Considerable
% of all health care costs paid by patients	12	n.a.	8	6	27
Physician payments	Negotiated fees for ambulatory care; salaries for hospital physicians	Negotiated fee schedules	Salary	Salary (some capitation)	Primarily fee-for-service based on physician charges
Hospital payments	Negotiated per diem rates	Global budgets	Global budgets	Global budgets	Often based on reported costs or charges

n.a. = not available.
SOURCE: Adapted from Congressional Budget Office, *Physician Reimbursement under Medicare* (April 1986), Appendix A.

higher in the United States than elsewhere. Yet cost sharing is much more prevalent, and Americans pay much more of their medical bill than do patients in other countries. Americans pay more than one quarter of health care costs out of pocket, compared with only 12 percent in Germany and less than 8 percent in Sweden and the United Kingdom.

Economic differences are not the only differences displayed in table 3–5. The United States has a mixed, public-private system, which relies primarily on private insurance to finance health care provided by nongovernmental agencies. The U.S. health care system is least like those of Sweden and the United Kingdom, which provide universal protection through public health insurance. Another key difference is the manner in which physicians and hospitals are paid for their services. The United States has traditionally reimbursed providers for incurred or expected costs. Although it is now shifting to fixed payments, it uses them less than other countries, which rely on negotiated rates or preset budgets. These financing differences derive from more fundamental divergences in health policy.

Some clues to the role of politics in the pricing and delivery of health care emerge from a comparison of the United States and Canada, neighboring countries with similar orientations to medical training and hospital care. One would expect these countries to be alike in health care costs and coverage. In fact, from 1950 to 1970, both countries had identical inflation rates in health care prices.[7] In 1965 both the United States and Canada spent 6.1 percent of GDP on health care. Shortly after the United States initiated Medicare and Medicaid, Canada adopted its own Federal Medical Care Act.

Since 1970, health care spending has accelerated in both countries, but at quite different rates. As a percentage of GDP, Canada's health care spending rose only 0.1 percent during the 1970s. During the same decade, however, U.S. spending climbed from 7.6 percent of GDP to 9.5 percent. Since 1980 the share of GDP spent on health care has increased in both countries, but it still is significantly lower in Canada than in the United States. The different trends have been due to decisions of Canadian governments to constrain charges, capacity, and utilization.[8] These political decisions have enabled Canada to provide universal coverage at a cost lower than that of the more limited protection available in the United States.

Politics interacts with economics and a broad range of social and cultural variables to shape each country's health policies and finances. The next section identifies some characteristics of American politics that result in high expenditures and limited coverage.

Political Influences on Health Policy

Politics influences health care at two levels. First, core values pervade the political system and shape public expectations about government policy. Second, these values are translated into policy by the behavioral patterns of politics. This discussion is necessarily brief and incomplete. It is intended to suggest avenues of inquiry, not to provide firm answers to the problems vexing health policy.

Political Values. One country may dispense health care as a right to which all persons are entitled regardless of financial circumstance; another may treat it as a commodity that is freely exchanged at market prices. The first country values equality, the second gives primacy to free enterprise. These values collide in all democratic countries. Through much of its history, however, the United States had mitigated conflict between them by conceiving of enterprise as the primary way to expand equality.

Enterprise has long been the dominant value in providing and financing medical care in the United States. One sees the spirit of enterprise in the role of the physician as a small businessman who charges for services rendered, in the extensive marketing of private health insurance, in the fee-for-service basis of financing hospital care, and in the billions of payments patients make each year for drugs and physicians' services. Equality has been a recent arrival on the American health scene. Its principal manifestation is in the Medicare-Medicaid financing of health care for the elderly and the needy.

The late attention to equality did not displace the established enterprise system for providing and paying for medical services. Modeling its behavior on preexisting insurance arrangements, the federal government took on the role of third-party payer for services requested or furnished by others. Cost reimbursement remained the basis for paying hospitals, and doctors continued to charge their customary fees.

The grafting of equity objectives onto the medical enterprise system has resulted in the mixture of public and private roles that distinguishes American health care from that of other major democracies (see table 3–5). The mixed system reflects the American yearning to have the best of both values: equal access without intrusion on the capacity of providers and users to make their own choices. Table 3–5 shows how this posture differs from that of four other countries. All the others have more vigorously pursued equality, even at the price of curtailing enterprise in health care. Canada and Germany have opted for considerably more price and service regulation than is imposed in the United States. Sweden and the United Kingdom have sought equality by operating their own national health services, which severely constrain the scope for enterprise.[9]

Whatever its strengths, the American mixture of enterprise and equality generates higher costs and provides more limited coverage than the systems in other countries. To control costs, a country must ration access to health care or make surplus providers compete by lowering prices. An enterprising country allows the market to ration access. It lowers overall spending on health by denying care to those who cannot afford it. An equalizing country rations by government decree. It constrains costs by denying certain services to both the poor and the nonpoor.[10] In seeking to have it both ways, the American mixture of public and private roles manifests reluctance to restrict the health care market while enhancing access by those unable to pay market prices.

This mixed system drives up costs in two ways: first, by allowing enterprising providers to render and charge for services as they deem appropriate; second, by making third-party payers foot the bill for the actions of others. To control costs, this mixed system must ration access, by either limiting the services provided or restricting eligibility for the services. This has not been easy because rationing by regulation would inhibit enterprise and rationing by denying coverage might violate equality.

Trapped between these widely held values, "many American physicians, as well as government, business and other leaders, have publicly rejected explicit rationing." Instead, the United States practices what Howard Hiatt has called "rationing by default."[11] This type of rationing occurs when access to health insurance is linked to employment, when the market prices many elderly out of long-term-care facilities, and when hospitals do not admit patients who lack third-party coverage. The United States also has explicit rationing, such as limitations on Medicare-Medicaid eligibility and coverage, and various regulations affecting the provision of health care like those related to hospital construction or expansion.

Rationing reduces the nation's health care expenditures substantially, but costs are still much higher than they would be if either core value were abandoned. Conversely, health protection is more limited than it would be if costs were lower and more people could therefore afford health care services.

The tension between enterprise and equality presents American health policy makers with difficult choices. If they seek to remedy the inadequate coverage problem, they risk further cost escalation. If they seek to control costs, they will be pressured to further constrict coverage. This dilemma is discussed in the final section.

Political Behavior

A number of the political system's behavioral characteristics influence health policy. Some features discussed here are peculiar to health policy; others are found more broadly in American politics. The following four features bear on the value conflict between enterprise and equality and on the cost-coverage problem: (1) the government's third-party role; (2) distributive politics; (3) incremental policy making; and (4) changing programs through budget decisions.

The Government as Third Party. The federal government became the third party in the health care system when it established Medicare and Medicaid. This role derived from the government's determination not to disturb the medical enterprise when it sought to enhance equality by providing financial aid to the elderly and the poor.

In politics, as in other social relations, third parties are inherently weak. The third party does not directly participate in decisions affecting its interests; it becomes involved only in the aftermath of these decisions. The role of government as third-party payer has a number of consequences for health care. First, this role (along with other factors) defines health care issues in financial rather than programmatic terms. For the payer, the pressing public policy concerns are what can be done to lower costs, who should pay for benefits, what should be done to slow inflation in the health sector, and the like. When resources are plentiful, the government can consider program issues such as the quality of, or access to, health care, along with financing questions. But substantive policy issues tend to get crowded out when the budget is tight and the government is pressured to cut expenditures.

Second, the government's distance from program decisions can be an advantage when it seeks cutbacks. Because it is not directly involved in these decisions, the government can be ignorant of the effects of financing changes on the provision of medical services. It can, for example, alter reimbursement formulas, freeze physician fees, or delay payments without full awareness of how these actions affect providers or beneficiaries. In so doing, the government as third party can claim to be cutting expenditures, not service levels.

Third, the distance and ignorance of the government can lead to unintended, possibly perverse, side effects. When the government,

41

as the uninvolved third party, cuts Medicare or Medicaid, it cannot be sure how much will be saved or what program changes will result. It might find coverage shrinking without comparable reductions in costs. There is reason to believe that some of the federal government's recent financing actions have caused behavioral changes that have significantly reduced the actual savings. Cost controls can lead to higher first-day charges for Medicare patients and to congressional caps on increases in these charges. They can spur increase of testing, patient dumping, efforts by the elderly to conceal assets, shifts of Medicare patients to Medicaid rolls, and so on.

Its third-party role can offer the government only a temporary respite from attempts to balance enterprise and equality. Sooner or later, the program effects of financing decisions become apparent. Some already have in the form of "quicker and sicker" stories, patient dumping exposés, and studies showing that shrinking coverage to the poor and unprotected has spawned more inequality in health care. The next stage in the balancing of competing values will push the federal government to a more active and direct role than that of third party.

Redistributive Politics. The preference for equality without disturbing the health enterprise manifests a key behavioral norm of American politics—distribute benefits, avoid redistributive policies. Distributive politics are evident in the enactment of Medicare and Medicaid, which gave benefits to the aged and the poor without taking away the benefits of private care enjoyed by doctors, hospitals, and other patients. Patients could select their own physician and purchase the services they wanted. Hospitals continued to be paid their costs and physicians, their charges.

The distributive character of health programs was facilitated by open-ended financing arrangements. From the start, Medicare obligated the government to pay the full amounts to which providers and recipients were entitled. Additional consumption of health care by some patients did not diminish the services to which others were entitled; they only added to total program costs. Spending was not controlled by budget decisions. If utilization or costs were higher than expected, the government paid the additional amounts.

As health care costs mounted and overall budget stress intensified, the federal government was faced with pressure for redistribution. One possibility would have been to target Medicare to less affluent patients; another, to reduce coverage or raise premiums. But to avoid explicit redistribution, the government made cutbacks in financial terms, such as freezing payment levels and shifting to prospective payment for inpatient care. When, because of these types of decisions, some patients were released early, it was the hospitals, not the federal government, that denied them services. Similarly, when first-day charges rose because of lower hospital utilization (which, in turn, was partly a consequence of prospective payment), the added out-of-pocket costs were not explicitly mandated by the government. By veiling the redistributive effects of its financing decisions, the government has encouraged "rationing by default," which does most injury to those who can least afford to pay for health care. It is highly unlikely that the government intended that an increasing percentage of low-income children be unprotected by Medicaid or that uninsured patients be released by hospitals. These have, however, been some of the perverse effects of federal health policy.

The avoidance of explicit redistribution has hobbled the government's capacity to remedy inadequacies in health care protection. Unless the government were willing to spend a lot more on health care, significant expansion of coverage for some patients would have to be financed by cutbacks in services or increased charges for others. The task of redistribution is even more difficult when the losers outnumber the winners, which would occur if improvements in Medicare's long-term care were financed by cutting services to all aged Americans.

As difficult as it is to undertake, explicit redistribution is on the horizon for federally financed health care. Cost pressures and growing evidence that many of the elderly are relatively well off will spur redistribution. If a means test for Medicare benefits is politically infeasible, there will be other ways to accomplish the same objective, such as by taxing these benefits or basing premiums on ability to pay.[12]

Incrementalism. The federal government is a health care incrementalist. Incrementalism has predisposed the government to build on existing institutions and practices and to avoid jarring changes that would disturb powerful interests. Wilbur Cohen, the leading architect of the Medicare-Medicaid legislation, has written of that measure: "The merits of the incremental approach [were] always in the forefront of my mind." He saw that legislation "as part of a long-term process—a continuation from the past, a creation in a particular moment of time, an incremental evolution for the future."[13]

As far-reaching as the 1965 law was, it was guided by incremental norms. Key features of the existing fee-for-service, cost-reimbursement system were retained. The insurance industry was recruited to administer Medicare, Medicaid was linked to state-run Aid to Families with Dependent Children (AFDC) programs, and the established means of paying hospitals and doctors were kept intact.

The "reasonable cost" principle was explicitly endorsed in the 1965 provision. It specified that, in devising reimbursement methods, the government should consider "the principles generally applied by national organizations or established prepayment organizations."[14]

While one face of incrementalism looks to past practices, the other looks to the expansion of programs along the path already taken. The original Medicaid law contained the seed of expansion. It directed the government to withhold payments from any state failing to make satisfactory "efforts in the direction of broadening of the scope of the care . . . and in the direction of liberalizing the eligibility requirements for medical assistance, with a view toward furnishing by July 1, 1975, comprehensive care and services to substantially all individuals who meet the plan's eligibility standards . . . including services to enable such individuals to attain or retain independence or self-care."[15]

In its early years Medicare was expanded modestly, most notably to victims of end-stage renal disease. Incremental expansion was abetted by underestimation of (or inattention to) the added costs, as well as by the buildup of surpluses in the Medicare trust fund. During the 1970s, however, fiscal pressures intensified, and it was not possible to disregard the growing burden on government budgets. Incrementalism was halted in its track. The 1974 drive for national health insurance was stymied by cost concerns, and Congress (at the behest of some states) repealed the Medicaid requirement that states liberalize benefits.

With incremental expansion blocked, Medicare and Medicaid coverage are today, even with improved protection against catastrophic illness, remarkably similar to what they were when these programs were launched. But the halt of incrementalism could not constrain the rise in health expenditures. Consequently, the government embarked almost a decade ago on decremental actions to control rising costs. Medicaid eligibility has been tightened; this program now covers fewer of the poor than it did in the early 1980s. Decrementalism is a form of incremental behavior: continuation on the selected path and small, piecemeal adjustments, but no reconsideration of basic policies.

When financial pressures induced decremental behavior, the conflict between enterprise and equality became more pronounced and health policy was paralyzed. The two principal health care initiatives of the 1970s—national health insurance and hospital cost

44

containment—failed. The former would have brought the goal of equal health care much closer to realization; the latter would have infringed on free markets. These outcomes can be seen as the triumph of enterprise over equality, or of the status quo over big changes. Whatever the interpretation, the legacy has been the anomaly that is the theme of this chapter: inadequate coverage at high cost.

Financing Decisions. When cost pressures turned incrementalism into decremental behavior, they also altered the form of policy decisions. Incremental decisions tend to be made in program legislation, decremental ones in budget measures. When programs are being expanded, policy makers highlight the additional benefits to be provided. Medicare and Medicaid were established in substantive legislation. The current drive to cover catastrophic illness is following the same path. But when the emphasis is on trimming expenditures, issues are defined in financial terms and decided in budget measures that veil the program consequences of the cuts.

Some of the characteristics of these measures are summarized here.[16] Budget measures, such as reconciliation bills, put a premium on short-term savings that reduce spending or the deficit. This objective is often accomplished by freezes, changes in the timing of payments, and other financing adjustments that save money without openly tampering with program coverage or eligibility. The savings are measured against an inflated baseline, which enables politicians to take credit for reducing the deficit even when health expenditures continue to rise.

The recurring budget cutbacks—six reconciliation measures have been enacted since 1980—encourage numerous piecemeal changes. According to one count, the 1986 Consolidated Omnibus Budget Reconciliation Act (COBRA) P.L. 99-272 made fifty-one changes in Medicare.[17] Dozens of additional changes were enacted later in the same year by the Omnibus Budget Reconciliation Act (OBRA) P.L. 99-509. Many of these were temporary provisions that saved money without altering the structure of Medicare.

Nothing Can Be Done about the Problem; Something Has to Be Done

Can the decremental practices of recent years persist? At first blush, the answer appears to be yes. The decremental cuts have eased the short-term financial crisis without significantly reducing coverage. Just a few years ago, Medicare's hospital insurance trust fund was at the brink of depletion; more recent projections show that it will remain solvent into the next century.[18] As long as politicians can postpone the bad news without making redistributive trade-offs or harsh cutbacks, they will.

But despite its apparent success, decrementalism cannot be sustained. One problem is that marginal cutbacks will not halt the rise in the portion of national output spent on health care. Another is that pressure is building up to expand public financing of medical services. In short, decrementalism does not do enough to control costs, nor does it permit expansion of coverage.

The main cost pressures will come from increases in the number of aged, especially the very old. By the year 2010, the United States will have 10 million more persons age sixty-five and over than it now has. By 2035, there will be almost 40 million more. Most of this increase will occur among those age seventy-five and older.[19] The utilization of health care services increases with age. People seventy-five and over account for about 15 percent of all hospital days, almost four times their proportion of the population. Those eighty-five and older have almost double the hospital utilization rate of the group age sixty-five to sixty-nine.[20] As the number of elderly Americans grows, the revenue base of Medicare will shrink in relative size. By the middle of the next century, the ratio of active workers to Medicare enrollees will be halved from more than 4:1 to barely 2:1.[21]

Decrementalism also has limited staying power because public support is building to improve coverage. Despite soaring costs, there is widespread belief that Medicare and Medicaid have borne more than their fair share of budget cuts. The frequent tampering with Medicare and Medicaid rules has left providers and recipients with the impression that truly deep cuts have been made. In fact, the actual cuts have almost certainly been less than half of the $30 billion or more alleged to have been taken from these programs in the 1980s.

In terms of public perception, however, it does not matter that the cutbacks have been exaggerated. In a 1987 public opinion poll, 75 percent favored an increase in Medicare (a higher percentage than for any of the ten other federal programs surveyed), and 61 percent endorsed an increase in Medicaid.[22] The pent-up demand for improved coverage has led to the enactment of a catastrophic illness program in the Congress. This expansion will set the stage for the next round, when long-term institutional care might be on the table.

The United States faces two alternative health care futures. If the high cost–low coverage anomaly persists, costs will escalate, but millions of Americans will still lack adequate protection. The alternative scenario is one in which the inexorable rise in costs is accompanied by major improvements in health coverage. Note that in both futures, health costs will consume a significantly higher share of GNP than is now the case. In view of past performance and projected demographic trends, it is highly implausible to think of stable health care expenditures in the decades ahead.

There may be an advantage in bowing to the inevitability of higher health care spending in the future. If it is recognized that health care expenditures will rise to 13–15 percent of GNP,[23] then analysts and politicians can think about alternative ways of spending the additional hundreds of billions of dollars that will be available for health care. They need not be wedded to incremental solutions. Instead, they can seek bolder changes in the health care system than might otherwise be made.

The added spending can buy either of the futures outlined above: inadequate, though somewhat expanded, coverage at higher cost, or improved protection obtained through higher expenditure. If the political values and behavior discussed here continue to dominate health policy, the first of these futures will come to pass, and the anomaly of high costs and low coverage will become more pervasive and less tractable.

It is easy to outline a better health care system than we now have. The ingredients would surely include expanded protection for the poor and uninsured, tighter control of costs, more assistance for those needing long-term care, and better targeting of Medicare benefits. These prescriptions add up to more equality at the price of less enterprise. Americans have generally been unwilling to pay this price in the past. They have opted for more equality only when they also preserved initiative and independence.

Why should they be willing to pay this price in the future? It is likely that the medical enterprise will be altered by cost pressures even if access to care is not significantly equalized. As health care costs continue to spiral, there will be more regulation and intrusion by government. Seen from this perspective, the choice is not between equality and enterprise, but between more or less equality in the provision of health care. In either case, medical enterprise will be constrained by financial pressures and changes in government policies.

The rest of this discussion examines changes that may occur in the political values and behavior discussed earlier.

Equality. Imagine a country spending almost 15 percent of its gross national product on health care, but denying ready access to this care to almost 15 percent of its population. This prospect may well materialize if cost and coverage trends continue along the lines of past developments.

The most pressing need in the equalization of access to health care is giving every American, as a matter of right, protection through a federal health insurance program covering basic medical services.[24] The more than 35 million Americans lacking health insurance are much weaker politically than the almost 30 million who have Medicare. But the case for giving universal health insurance priority over long-term care for the elderly is compelling.

First, it is unjust to divide the country into haves and have-nots, and it is cruel for an affluent nation to permit conditions that give rise to patient dumping. Further, universal health care coverage is a less costly innovation than long-term care. Indeed, it can be argued that the United States might now be spending less on health care if it had opted for one of the health insurance options rejected in the past. Finally, offering universal health insurance would affect the medical enterprise less than extending Medicare coverage to long-term care. One reason is that the U.S. health care system is already structured around insurance programs. Another is that public financing of long-term care would alter the expectations and behavior of the elderly, their families, and providers.

Constrained Enterprise. Adoption of a long-term-care entitlement would be extremely expensive under the best of circumstances, but prohibitively so if the United States fails to slow the growth in health care costs. To control costs, it will be necessary for the government to infringe on medical enterprise.[25] It will do so in ways that preserve both core values, but tilt the emphasis toward more equality at the expense of a bit less enterprise. Within a constrained health care system, there still will be enormous scope for enterprise.

In balancing these values, radical solutions like a national health service will be as distasteful to Americans as they always have been. Instead, the infringement on enterprise will come about through government-maintained constraints on both the supply of and demand for medical services. There will be more explicit rationing of health care, more regulated or negotiated prices, and tougher mandatory assignment rules. Some of these changes might evolve without the strong arm of government controls, as providers, patients, and insurers grapple for new ways to deliver care. The evolution might lead to some demedicalization of institutional care for the elderly and more reliance on intermediate-care facilities that are less costly than hospitals.

Beyond a Third-Party Role. Constraints on enterprise will move the federal government beyond the role of third-party payer. While the government will remain the primary financing source of health care for low-income and elderly Americans, it also will play a more active role as regulator and negotiator. It will not, however, provide health care in any substantial degree.

No matter how successful the government is as a negotiator or regulator, it will have to allocate a rising portion of the federal budget to health care financing. As this share rises, government will be pressured to intercede more directly and vigorously in the health care market. It will also hear counterarguments that deregulation will enable the market to ration and price health care efficiently. Increased regulation may therefore be followed by periods of deregulation. But unless costs recede as a health care problem, the long-term trend will be toward more government involvement in the market.

More Redistribution. The case for redistributing the costs and benefits of health care rests on two premises. First, without redistribution, health care costs will soar to unacceptable levels. Second, a growing portion of the elderly have sufficient assets to contribute substantial amounts to their health care. Although redistribution is always difficult in American politics, it is somewhat easier to accomplish by changing the tax code than by taking away middle-class entitlements. Thus, the Congress that was unwilling to cut social security benefits significantly was willing to impose a tax on a portion of these benefits. Similarly, Congress has recently enacted differential Medicare premiums based on income. Americans are accustomed to graduated tax rates, but they seem unwilling to condition Medicare eligibility on income.

Because of the aversion to targeting Medicare benefits, redistribution can be better accomplished by providing income assistance to the aged poor through Supplemental Security Income (SSI) than by establishing a means test for entitlement to health benefits. Adding a few billion dollars to SSI would do more to boost the income of the needy elderly than adding an equivalent amount to Medicare.

Some Nonincremental, Non-budget-driven Policies. Incrementalism is so deeply rooted in our political behavior that it will continue to dominate policy making. We will avoid a major reconsideration of policy as long as possible. If Medicare remains solvent or can be sustained by politically acceptable transfers from the social security fund, Congress will persist in its incremental ways, enacting periodic expansions while continuing to make decremental adjustments through budget-driven legislation, as it has in recent years.

HICKSVILLE PUBLIC LIBRARY
HICKSVILLE, N.Y.

Perhaps a consideration of universal health insurance or of long-term care will spur a thorough examination of health policy. But the new catastrophic illness legislation has not served this purpose, nor might more far-reaching expansions in health care.

Increment by increment the United States has moved from spending 6 percent of its output on health care to spending 11 percent. This escalation was accomplished in only twenty years, a remarkably short period. The lesson of incrementalism, as in the fable of the hare and the tortoise, is that a lot of ground can be covered by taking small steps. A continuation of this incremental trend would leave the United States twenty years hence with even higher costs and still inadequate coverage. At that time, we will wonder how we got into the mess and whether we can do anything to get out of it.

Notes

1. These data cover total spending—public and private. See Daniel R. Waldo, Katharine R. Levit, and Helen Lazenby, "National Health Expenditures, 1985," *Health Care Financing Review*, vol. 8 (Fall 1986), pp. 1–15.

2. A 1984 report of the Senate Special Committee on Aging estimated out-of-pocket health care costs at 15 percent of mean income of the elderly in both 1966 and 1984. For the relationship between income and these expenditures, see Marian Gornick and others, "Twenty Years of Medicare and Medicaid: Covered Populations, Use of Benefits, and Program Expenditures," *Health Care Financing Review*, 1985 Annual Supplement, pp. 52–53.

3. The 1986 data are preliminary; final figures might show a different inflation rate. The data with respect to hospital profits are controversial, and various studies have reported different profit margins. See the *New York Times*, March 29, 1987, p. 1.

4. There are a number of ways of measuring Medicaid's coverage of the low-income population, and each method yields different results. The Census Bureau's Annual Population Survey found that in 1983 only 38.7 percent of the population below the poverty level had Medicaid coverage sometime during the year. The 1980 National Medical Care Utilization and Expenditure Survey reported that 49 percent of the poverty population had Medicaid coverage. The ratio of Medicaid recipients to the poverty population has steeply declined from .92 in 1977 to only .64 in 1984. See Gornick and others, "Twenty Years of Medicare," p. 34.

5. In 1985, the per capita Medicaid payment for dependent children receiving assistance was $453; the per capita payment for aged recipients was $4,605. See Committee on Ways and Means, U.S. House of Representatives, *Background Material and Data on Programs within the Jurisdiction of the Committee on Ways and Means*, 1987 edition, p. 310.

6. See Organization for Economic Cooperation and Development, *Measuring Health Care 1960–1983: Expenditure, Costs, and Performance* (Paris: OECD, 1985).

7. See T. R. Marmor, *Medicare at Age 20: Its Past, Present, and Future* (Project on the Federal Social Role, 1985), pp. 6–7.

8. For a succinct description of the Canadian health care system, see Howard H. Hiatt, *America's Health in the Balance* (New York: Harper & Row, 1987), pp. 111–19.

9. Victor R. Fuchs, citing a number of British economists, argues that the National Health Service "was created primarily in pursuit of the goal of equality." See *The Health Economy* (Cambridge, Mass.: Harvard University Press, 1986), p. 291.

10. Ibid., p. 25. Fuchs argues that the goal of reducing inequality of access to medical care "may require rationing the amount available to the nonpoor as well as subsidizing the poor. One economist has argued that the British approach to health care through a national health service can best be understood in these terms."

11. The term is taken from Hiatt, who entitles the first chapter of this book, "Rationing by Default." Hiatt, *America's Health in the Balance*, p. 8.

12. The catastrophic health care legislation enacted in 1988 ties a portion of Medicare premiums to the income of recipients.

13. Wilbur J. Cohen, "Reflections on the Enactment of Medicare and Medicaid," in *Health Care Financing Review*, 1985 Annual Supplement, p. 10.

14. Section 1861(v) of the Social Security Amendments of 1965, P.L. 89–97. Title XVIII of this law established the Medicare program.

15. Section 1903(e) of the Social Security Amendments of 1965, P.L. 89–97. Title XIX of this law established the Medicaid program.

16. See also, Allen Schick, "Controlling the 'Uncontrollables': Budgeting for Health Care in an Age of Megadeficits," in Jack A. Meyer and Marion Ein Lewin, eds., *Charting the Future of Health Care* (Washington, D.C.: American Enterprise Institute, 1987), pp. 13–34.

17. See Committee on Ways and Means, *Background Material*, p. 170ff.

18. *1987 Annual Report of the Board of Trustees of the Federal Hospital Insurance Trust Fund*, March 30, 1987, p. 9. This projection is based on the board's alternative II-B (intermediate) assumptions. More optimistic assumptions project the fund's solvency at least until 2013; more pessimistic assumptions would have the fund insolvent in 1996.

19. These demographic projections are based on Bureau of the Census, *Projections of the Population of the United States by Age, Sex, and Race: 1983 to 2080*, Publication P-25, no. 952 (Washington, D.C.: Government Printing Office, 1984).

20. U.S. General Accounting Office, *Elderly Needs and Costs* (GAO/HRD 86–135, 1986), p. 33.

21. Federal Hospital Insurance Trust Fund, *Annual Report of the Board of Trustees*, 1987, p. 11.

22. Washington Post–ABC News Poll, reported in the *Washington Post*, January 27, 1987.

23. A recent unpublished projection by the Health Care Financing Administration estimates that the cost of health care will rise to 15 percent of GNP by the year 2000.

24. A compellingly eloquent case for universal insurance is made by

Professor Uwe E. Reinhardt in a statement, "Rationing the Nation's Health Care Surplus: A Paradox? or as American as Apple Pie?" before the House Select Committee on Aging, September 12, 1986.

25. Henry J. Aaron and William B. Schwartz, *The Painful Prescription: Rationing Hospital Care* (Washington, D.C.: Brookings Institution, 1984).

4
Economic Growth and
the Health Care Budget

John H. Makin

A study by the International Monetary Fund shows that, over the past twenty-five years, government expenditure on health and medical care has more than doubled as a share of gross national product (GNP) in seven major industrial countries. At the same time, the share of health care spending directed to the elderly population over age sixty-five has risen far more rapidly than the proportion of that group in the total population. Since the average cost of medical care per person rises sharply after age sixty-five, most indexes show that the overall cost of care has risen rapidly, partly because more has been directed to the over-sixty-five population. Other factors, such as qualitative changes in a "unit" of health care, have also caused health care costs to rise far more rapidly than average prices.

All these trends are especially noticeable in the United States. In 1985 direct U.S. health care spending was 10.7 percent of GNP, or $425 billion. That figure is of an order of magnitude equal to such other spending aggregates as total imports, total nonresidential investment, or three times all personal saving. Table 4–1 displays aggregate statistics on U.S. health expenditures.

Between 1965 and 1985, GNP grew fivefold, while spending on health care grew tenfold. If that trend were to continue, as of course it will not, a male child born in 1988 with a life expectancy of seventy-one years would see all GNP devoted to health care spending at the time of his actuarial death. These figures are just another way of saying that pressures to reduce the growth in spending on health care will increase. The preferred way to slow the growth in such spending is to reduce the cost of health care services. It is primarily a rise in the relative price of health care services, rather than faster growth in the real supply of those services, that has accounted for increased health care spending as a share of GNP over the past twenty years.

The rise in the price of health care services, relative to both the consumer price index (CPI) and the services component of the CPI,

53

TABLE 4-1
NATIONAL HEALTH EXPENDITURES: SELECTED CALENDAR YEARS, 1965–1985

	1965	1967	1970	1975	1980	1981	1982	1983	1984	1985
Billions of dollars										
National health expenditures	41.9	51.5	75.0	132.7	248.1	287.0	323.6	357.2	390.2	425.0
Private	30.9	32.5	47.2	76.4	142.9	165.8	188.4	209.7	230.7	250.2
Public	11.0	19.0	27.8	56.3	105.2	121.2	135.3	147.5	159.5	174.8
Federal	5.5	11.9	17.7	37.0	71.0	83.3	93.2	102.7	111.7	124.4
State and local	5.5	7.0	10.1	19.3	34.2	37.9	42.1	44.8	47.8	50.4
Dollars per capita										
National health expenditures	205	247	349	590	1,054	1,207	1,348	1,473	1,595	1,721
Private	152	156	220	340	607	697	784	865	943	1,013
Public	54	91	129	250	447	510	563	608	652	708
Federal	27	57	82	165	302	350	388	424	456	504
State and local	27	34	47	86	145	159	175	185	195	204
Percentage distribution										
National health expenditures	100.0	100.0	100.0	100.0	100.0	100.0	100.0	100.0	100.0	100.0
Private	73.8	63.2	63.0	57.5	57.6	57.8	58.2	58.7	59.1	58.9
Public	26.2	36.8	37.0	42.5	42.4	42.2	41.8	41.3	40.9	41.1
Federal	13.2	23.2	23.6	27.9	28.6	29.0	28.8	28.8	28.6	29.3
State and local	13.0	13.7	13.5	14.5	13.8	13.2	13.0	12.5	12.3	11.9

Average annual percentage change from previous year shown

U.S. population	—	1.1	1.0	0.9	1.0	1.0	1.0	1.0	0.9	0.9
Gross national product	—	7.6	7.5	9.5	8.9	11.7	3.7	7.4	11.0	5.7
National health expenditures	—	10.8	13.4	12.1	15.6	15.7	12.8	10.4	9.2	8.9
Private	—	2.5	13.3	10.1	15.1	16.0	13.6	11.3	10.0	8.5
Public	—	31.3	13.6	15.2	16.2	15.2	11.6	9.1	8.1	9.6
Federal	—	46.7	14.0	16.0	16.4	17.3	11.9	10.2	8.7	11.4
State and local	—	13.6	12.8	13.8	15.8	10.9	11.1	6.4	6.8	5.3
Number in millions										
U.S. population[a]	204.1	208.6	215.1	224.9	235.3	237.8	240.2	242.5	244.7	246.9
Billions of dollars										
Gross national product	705	816	1,015	1,598	2,732	3,053	3,166	3,402	3,775	3,989
Percentage of gross national product										
National health expenditures	5.9	6.3	7.4	8.3	9.1	9.4	10.2	10.5	10.3	10.7

NOTE: Numbers may not add to 100 because of rounding.

a. July 1 social security area population estimates.

SOURCE: Health Care Financing Administration, Office of the Actuary: Data from the Division of National Cost Estimates.

TABLE 4–2
ANNUAL INCREASE IN COST OF MEDICAL SERVICES RELATIVE TO
CONSUMER PRICE INDEX AND TO NONMEDICAL SERVICES, 1965–1985
(percent)

Years	Costs Relative to CPI	Cost Relative to Nonmedical Services	Economic Real Growth
1965–1985	33.3	16.7	2.7
1975–1985	29.2	9.4	2.9
1980–1985	56.4	22.9	2.4

NOTE: Calculated as average annual percentage increase in medical services divided by average annual percentage increase in CPI or nonmedical services.
SOURCE: Department of Labor, Bureau of Labor Statistics.

has persisted (see table 4–2). Between 1965 and 1985, prices of medical care services rose on average one-third faster than the CPI and about 17 percent faster than the index for nonmedical care services. The trend toward higher relative prices for medical services has become more pronounced in the 1980s, as such prices are rising more than 50 percent faster than the CPI and 23 percent faster than nonmedical services.

There appears to be a downward rigidity in the growth of health care costs. Normally, when the economy slows, inflation slows too; this is less true for medical services. For the years covered by table 4–2 (1965–1985), the *relative* cost of medical services rose more rapidly when output grew more slowly, or, put more directly, medical care in the United States has tended to get more expensive when we can least afford it. On the positive side, faster growth of output tends to slow the rise in the relative cost of health care services. The price of medical services seems to rise steadily, unaffected by market forces that affect prices of other goods and services.

A rise in the cost of health care services relative to other goods, coupled with an increase in the share of health care spending on the over-sixty-five population, implies that the pattern of health care spending carries with it a transfer of resources from young to old. Perhaps more than any other single issue, the changing pattern of health care expenditure worldwide, and especially in the United States over the past twenty years, has important implications for generational equity.

Public Spending on Health Care

Between 1965 and 1985, the fastest-growing component of health care spending was public sector expenditure. The average annual growth rate of government spending on health care during this period was 14.8 percent, with federal spending rising at a rate of 16.9 percent. These figures largely reflect the impact of Medicare and Medicaid, America's relatively new "national health program."

The rising costs of health care programs and the role of the federal government in financing them will inevitably become an issue in the continuing national debate over budget deficits. Since 1981, deficits have added over $1 trillion to the national debt. Though controversial, the impact of an increase in the ratio of debt to GNP is not widely hailed as a positive development for the economy and many, including myself, would argue that the effect has been harmful. Slower economic growth is a fact of the 1980s, which means fewer resources for everything—including health care. Furthermore, because the real cost of health care tends to rise when economic growth slows, the burden of financing care increases when families are least able to manage it.

The ability of the federal government to finance discretionary changes to support health care programs is more limited than ever. Largely because of the trillion-dollar addition to the national debt over the past five years, federal receipts net of interest payments in 1986 were at their lowest level since 1951. After paying interest on the national debt, federal receipts in the postwar period have averaged 17.5 percent of GNP; in 1986, however, they were only 15.3 percent of GNP. That is well over $80 billion short of what would be available to spend on medical care and other government programs if the federal government were not so far in debt.

Increasing debt reduces the discretionary funds available to the federal government. Moreover, the government's increasing participation in funding health care also reduces discretionary funds available for non-health-care programs such as other entitlements, defense, education, and other discretionary programs. Merit aside, the political pressure to protect such programs is intense. Federal spending on health care in 1985 stood at $124.4 billion, or 29.3 percent of total spending for health care. If the federal share of total outlays had been 13.2 percent, as it was in 1965, federal spending for health care would have been reduced in 1985 by $56.2 billion. That is almost the amount required to meet the Gramm-Rudman-Hollings deficit target for fiscal year 1988. This is not to imply that federal health care programs should bear the brunt of budget cutting, but only to point out that other programs well below historical levels as a share of GNP are not susceptible to further large cuts.

Beyond direct spending on health care, the federal tax system provides massive subsidies that, like most tax preferences, favor high-income over low-income taxpayers. Exclusion of employer contributions for medical insurance premiums and medical care, deductibility of medical expenses, exclusion of interest on state and local government bonds for hospital facilities, and deductibility of charitable contributions for health cost the federal government about $26 billion of revenue in 1985. Because medical insurance is a nontaxable form of employee compensation, employers offer extensive medical benefits, which are more valuable to employees in higher tax brackets.

For an employee in the $200,000 income bracket, whose pre-1987 tax rate was 50 percent, a $3,000 medical plan was the equivalent of $6,000 before taxes. For an employee earning $20,000, who was in the 25 percent tax bracket, the same medical plan was equivalent to $4,000 before taxes. For both employees, the effect of excluding health insurance premiums from income was to increase the share of compensation earmarked as medical care, since that portion of his or her salary was not taxable. The effect, however, was regressive and less beneficial to low-income taxpayers because the value of the tax exclusion rose with tax rates.

The Tax Reform Act of 1986 mitigates the regressivity of fully deductible medical premiums by lowering the top marginal tax rate to 33 percent. This change means that even the employee earning more than $200,000 (actually in the 28 percent tax bracket) now finds that a $3,000 package of medical insurance is worth $4,167 in pre-tax income, rather than $6,000 as it was when the marginal tax rate was 50 percent. This is a good example of a primary aim of the Tax Reform Act of 1986. Lower marginal tax rates mean that tax preferences are less valuable and therefore less likely to distort choices of taxpayers and corporations.

Many have argued that, like homeownership, health care is for Americans a "sacred" category of expenditure that should be given tax preference. These arguments overlook the fact that tax preferences for homeownership and health care increase spending on those items. Consequently, their costs rise faster than the costs of other items that do not receive tax-favored treatment. In addition, the benefits of such policies are distributed regressively because their value rises directly in proportion to the marginal tax rate of the taxpayer enjoying them.

One way to encourage provision for adequate health insurance while minimizing the revenue loss associated with a tax preference would be to treat as taxable income any employer contributions for health insurance that exceed, for example, $200 a month for family coverage and $80 a month for individuals. According to the Congressional Budget Office (CBO), this "tax cap," which would do much to remove the regressive impact of the tax preference associated with health care, would add more than $36 billion to federal revenues between 1987 and 1991.

An even better alternative exists to cut regressivity and increase the ability of families and individuals to shop for the health plan best suited to their needs. All employer-paid health insurance premiums could be made taxable, but employees could be given tax credits of, for example, 25 percent of health insurance premiums up to $200 a month for families and $80 for individuals. This would be like giving a family $50 a month to buy whatever health plan it wished.

Since health plans would no longer be tax exempt, employers would be likely to stop offering them as part of compensation. Instead, they would be more likely to increase explicit salaries by the amount of the after-tax value of the health plan to the employee. Using their tax credits, employees could then purchase the amount and type of coverage they desire. This change would make plans far more responsive to individual needs and help to control costs. Families paying explicitly for health coverage would be as vigilant about watching costs and shopping for health care as they are concerning anything else they purchase.

According to the CBO, the tax credit provision would add nearly $60 billion to federal revenues by 1991. It would help contain health care costs by allowing each employee an equal basic credit to spend on health care as he or she chooses. This policy might help make health care costs more responsive to economic conditions and thereby help stem the rise in the relative price of health care services.

Pressure to reduce federal spending and the lower tax rates in the Tax Reform Act of 1986 will mean that federal resources available for funding health care will very likely grow more slowly than in the past. Meanwhile, the pressure on federal health care programs, especially Medicare and Medicaid, will increase sharply. These programs—particularly Medicare, which is aimed almost exclusively at the elderly—are beginning to suffer from the same demographic strains that will come to bear on the social security system in the twenty-first century. The ratio of costs (measured by the burden of payroll taxes on the working population) to benefits received by retirees is very low at first. But it rises exponentially, especially given the age profile of the American population.

It is important to understand a so-called demographic trap that plagues publicly funded programs in a population that will age rapidly as the postwar baby-boom generation begins to retire in twenty-five years. Consider a simple example. Imagine a society with the following demographics: ten children below working age, twenty working adults, and ten retirees. Payroll taxes for health care for retirees must be sufficient to provide $10 per year to each retiree, for a total of $100. In this situation, each worker pays $5 per year in taxes to support the retirees' health care program.

Suppose that in twenty years the demographics change as predicted so that there are ten children, ten workers and twenty retirees. In that situation, even if the health care cost per retiree remains at $10, each worker must be assessed $20 per year, or four times the original rate, to finance the program.

This is an oversimplified and somewhat exaggerated demographic example to illustrate that Medicare and other pay-as-you-go programs like social security are initially extremely attractive for the beneficiaries and not overly burdensome for working-age taxpayers. For a couple that retired in 1985, Medicare hospital insurance benefits will be anywhere from seven to twenty-six times the amount they paid in because the program was begun late in their working lives. The burden on future beneficiaries (who finance the program) is relatively light, since currently more than four covered workers support each Medicare enrollee. By the middle of the twenty-first century, however, that ratio will be cut in half. Even under the most optimistic assumptions, the Medicare trust fund will be exhausted well before this major demographic shift occurs, probably sometime during the 1990s and possibly as early as 1993 if pessimistic assumptions are realized.[1]

To sustain Medicare, the working-age population will have to pay considerably higher earmarked taxes. The intergenerational transfer implicit in the program will, in short, become far more obvious as the demographic trap victimizes an aging population.

The unsustainability of Medicare at current tax levels could easily have been foreseen. Demographic trends are highly predictable. Only the timing of a crisis is uncertain, because of uncertainty about the prospective rate of economic growth when the programs were enacted.

Indeed, one of the major difficulties for entitlement programs has been underperformance by the economy. During the 1960s when such programs were expanded, the general expectation for long-term economic growth was betwen 3.5 and 4 percent annually. The actual growth of output from 1965 through 1985, however, averaged only 2.7 percent per year. If it had averaged 4 percent, 1985 GNP would have been a trillion dollars larger than it was. Health care expenditures, at the 1985 level of $425 billion, would have been 8.3 percent of GNP instead of 10.7 percent. That we are well over $1 trillion short of the GNP envisioned when federal spending on health care programs was set on its present course will, along with the demographic trends that were fully predictable, force hard decisions on all areas of spending, including health care.

The question for government programs is whether they should be scaled back or the taxes earmarked to support them increased. The former option implies a reduction in the current level of transfers from young to old; the latter implies an increase.

The Returns to Health Care Spending

Surveying the statistics in the health care field, one realizes that almost all the numbers measure expenditures instead of the quality or quantity produced. Normally, people like to think more carefully about what they get for their money than they seem to when considering expenditures on health care. A rise in wages causes less concern, for example, if it is accompanied by a rise in labor productivity. And an increase in the average price of an automobile may be less troublesome because today, compared with ten years ago, the average automobile is lighter, has a fuel-injected engine, gets better mileage, has safer brakes, and probably is air-conditioned.

How do we measure the return on our "investment" represented by a doubling of the share of GNP devoted to health care over the past twenty years? The most readily available quantitative measures are life expectancy, mortality, and the presence or absence of chronic illness; labor productivity might also be relevant. The task is complicated by the difficulty in controlling for factors unrelated to direct expenditure on health care that may affect measures of life expectancy, infant mortality, or labor productivity. The quality of diet may improve regardless of direct expenditures on health care. People might exercise more or, on the negative side, suffer greater stress. More broadly, life expectancy may not increase, but the quality of life may improve over a given life span.

A look at life expectancy tables suggests that, between the early 1960s and 1982, there was a significant if uneven increase in life expectancy in the United States (see table 4–3). At birth, life expectancy for males and females has risen steadily, although the rate of increase for females since 1975 has slowed. For both males and females life expectancy at age forty has increased more rapidly than life expectancy at birth, although improvement for females slowed after 1975. Improved life expectancy at age forty is heartening. It suggests a significant lengthening of the expected useful lives of middle-aged adults that probably is due more to improved health care than to diet and exercise patterns, which tend to be well established by that age.

TABLE 4–3

LIFE EXPECTANCY IN THE UNITED STATES AND JAPAN, SELECTED YEARS,
1959–1985

		United States	
	1959–61	1975 (% rise since 1961)	1982 (% rise since 1975)
At birth			
Male	67.6	69.5 (2.8)	71.5 (2.9)
Female	74.2	77.3 (4.2)	78.8 (1.9)
Age 40			
Male	31.7	33.1 (4.4)	34.5 (4.2)
Female	37.1	39.5 (6.5)	40.6 (2.8)
Age 65			
Male	13.0	13.8 (6.2)	14.5 (5.0)
Female	15.9	18.2 (14.5)	18.9 (3.8)

		Japan	
	1960	1970 (% rise since 1960)	1985 (% rise since 1970)
At birth			
Male	65.3	69.3 (6.1)	74.8 (7.9)
Female	70.2	74.7 (6.4)	80.5 (7.8)

NOTE: U.S. data are for whites. Figures for blacks show similar improvement,
although life expectancies are lower.
SOURCE: *Statistical Abstract of the United States.*

The fastest rate of increase in life expectancy has come for males
and females at age sixty-five. This pattern is consistent with the
notion of a positive relationship between life expectancy and health
care expenditure, in view of the fact that in the United States such
expenditure has been heavily skewed toward the retired population.

Broadly interpreted, the life expectancy tables show that Americans in all age groups can expect longer lives than they could at the
beginning of the 1960s. Health expenditures skewed toward the
elderly (Medicare and part of Medicaid) have been accompanied by a
significant increase in life expectancy for people who are now sixty-
five. These observations suggest association but not necessarily cau-

sality. It would be interesting to devise quality-of-life indexes, particularly for people over sixty-five, to see whether we are getting what we hope for from significant real increases in health care expenditures on that age group.

Lest we become complacent, it is worth comparing the performance of the United States with other countries that spend less and differently on health care. National health expenditures in Japan, for example, have since 1960 averaged between 3 and 7 percent of GNP, or about half to two-thirds of U.S. levels. Yet life expectancy at birth has improved more rapidly there than in the United States. This may be because Japan's national health plan applies to all age groups rather than just to the elderly. Other factors such as diet, exercise habits, and levels of stress may explain the differences. Whatever the reasons, they deserve further study. International comparisons of health care expenditures and the tangible results, such as life expectancy, may provide some clues to identifying the pattern of health care expenditures that does most to improve the health of the population.

The life expectancy tables are only a snapshot measure of one "output" of health care spending. It might be useful to undertake a longitudinal study of life expectancy for two groups born twenty years apart, comparing figures at birth and throughout their lives in several countries where the pattern of spending on health differs and has changed over time. The major discretionary category of medical expenditure is that directed by government programs. Figure 4–1 displays dramatically how government programs in the United States have been directed toward the over-sixty-five population. The ratio of the share of government medical spending for the elderly to the portion of the population sixty-five and over is nearly four and a half times the same ratio for the under-fifteen population in the United States. In Japan the ratios are nearly equal because its national health program is directed at all age groups.

The distinction between health care expenditure as a form of investment in a durable and productive work force, as opposed to a form of consumption in expanding life during the retirement years, is more clearly drawn in less advanced economies than it is in the United States. An important question that longitudinal studies should answer is whether the unit cost of extending life and health in the post-retirement years can be reduced by spending more on health care or information about health care during childhood. This query amounts to a demographic version of the question about preventive versus curative medicine.

America's national health programs for the elderly, Medicare

FIGURE 4-1
RATIO OF THE SHARE OF GOVERNMENT MEDICAL EXPENDITURES TO THE
SHARE OF POPULATION

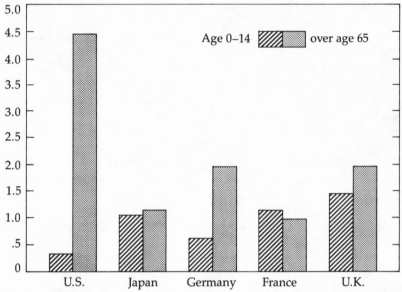

SOURCE: Author.

and part of Medicaid, demonstrate a strong commitment to meet
older Americans' health care needs. At the same time, much of the
middle class has been well provided for by treating employer-sponsored medical plans as nontaxable compensation. What is remarkable
is the absence of any national attention to the health needs of low-
income workers and children. Public assistance for the health of
children is tied to the vagaries of the welfare system. Low-income
workers are often in jobs for which employers do not believe they can
afford the high fixed cost of providing medical insurance or retirement benefits.

For middle- and low-income workers, a tax credit for health
insurance premiums would expand the choices available to include
more health plans, while eliminating these plans as a cost borne
directly by employers. Because the Tax Reform Act of 1986 was aimed
at removing many low-income taxpayers from the income tax rolls,
the credit might have to be allowed against social security payroll
taxes.

The proposal by Senator Edward Kennedy and others to require
employers to provide health insurance would only strengthen the
trend toward using temporary employees and would reduce employment opportunities for discretionary workers at the low end of the

pay scale. Such a proposal would be the equivalent of raising the minimum wage in the sense that it seems attractive but is counterproductive. Both result in higher labor costs and the substitution of more capital for labor. Moreover, high unit labor costs can be avoided in an increasingly integrated world economy by importing assembled components or by relocating production facilities abroad. We do not need policies that reduce incentives to produce more goods in the United States.

Summary and Conclusions

The American approach to improving health care for its population has been haphazard and designed to make real cost increases more likely. The typical consumer purchases health care either as part of an employment package or a welfare program, or as a counterpart to having reached retirement age. Individuals have almost no opportunity and usually little incentive to pay attention to the cost of the medical care they receive. It is therefore not surprising that medical care costs rise faster than the costs of goods and services for which consumers can "shop." If automobile insurance were designed like health insurance, automobile owners would obtain repairs and then submit their bills to the insurance company selected by their employers, rather than get estimates that clearly state the prospective cost of repairs to both the insured and the insurer.

The little attention we pay to the cost of medical care is a natural result of the value we place on human life. The question of how much health spending we can afford is often answered by saying that we must have as much as we need. Such a facile response avoids some difficult issues that must be confronted daily. Consider a simplified example of a group health insurance pool of 100 people who each pay in $300 a year. Suppose one member becomes seriously ill, and his life could be prolonged for one more week if the entire $30,000 in the pool were spent. The other members would then be left with zero health care resources for the rest of the year.

This painful example illustrates a point about health care, national defense, or any other high-priority category of expenditure. That we want as much as we need does not change the fact that resources are limited. Limited resources mean that spending more for one group leaves less for another.

Looking at this issue demographically raises fundamental questions about the stage in the life cycle at which increased health care spending has the greatest potential to improve longevity and quality of life for everyone. Will spending more on health care or spending more wisely during childhood improve life expectancy for a particular age group at significantly less cost than would be incurred by waiting until the group reaches sixty-five for some assured level of medical care? Put more directly, is preventive medicine more cost-effective than curative medicine and, if so, how can we redesign existing programs to emphasize prevention?

That choice has important intergenerational implications. We will soon face a choice regarding the financing of Medicare and Medicaid programs. The demographic trap will become painfully obvious in the 1990s as the ratio of retirees to workers begins to rise, while the real cost of medical services continues climbing steadily.

To contain spiraling medical costs, two approaches deserve serious attention. First, consumers of health care should have a greater choice in selecting providers. This could be accomplished by separating health care from employment through a universal tax credit for purchasing health plans. Second, consumers should be better educated about available health care plans and the benefits of healthier life styles. To expand consumer choices, individuals and families should receive adequate but equal health care tax credits. In effect, the government would say to a four-person family: "You have $50 a month to spend on health care. If you wish to spend more, you may do so but not at government expense." Individuals and families would then have a real incentive to find a health care plan that supplies the type and quality of care most suitable for them at a reasonable price.

The need to provide better education and information about health care to consumers has become almost a cliché, but it should not be neglected in the absence of widespread understanding of how important basic health practices are and of how to follow practices that lead to a healthier life style. Given restrictions on total resources available, increased efforts at prevention may imply the need for an intergenerational transfer in reverse—from old to young.

We have tended to assume that an economy as rich as ours ought to provide adequate health care for everyone in need. Indeed, that is probably a reasonable assumption. But if programs are so designed that the public is encouraged to consume health care without considering its cost or quality, eventually some adjustment will be needed. The day of reckoning will come sooner if the economy grows more slowly than anticipated by policy makers when they designed the existing collection of health care programs.

Government health care programs in the United States, unlike those in other countries, are directed toward the elderly. This raises questions about both intergenerational equity and the cost-effectiveness of health care spending. Retired Americans should expect to live reasonably healthy lives within the confines of age-related limitations and available resources. The question is whether a happy coincidence may exist concerning intergenerational allocation of health care expenditures. By directing health care resources more carefully to the young, can we reduce their care needs when they are middle-aged and elderly?

Note

1. These figures are from the Health Care Financing Administration, *Health Care Financing Review*, vol. 8, no. 1 (Fall 1986).

5
Can Rethinking
Some Fundamentals Make Old Age
More Productive and Satisfying?

Marvin H. Kosters

Increasing life expectancy is attributable in part to the growing sophistication of health care services. This has led to more policy attention devoted to issues in aging. The general goals of policy include satisfying, and even productive, lives during what have come to be thought of as retirement years; adequate income to support a decent or comfortable life style; access to health care when needed, while avoiding premature depletion of all the resources of the elderly; and reasonable arrangements to care for elderly who are extensively incapacitated or terminally ill.

Concerns about these goals and the costs of achieving them will surely grow in the future. Continuing gradual increases in the life expectancy of the elderly as well as advances in our ability to prolong life are likely. Even more important, however, will be the growing numbers of the elderly relative to the prime working-age population that will emerge early in the twenty-first century when the baby-boom generation begins to reach retirement age.

Current policy discussion about issues involving the elderly can probably best be characterized as concerns about filling gaps. The dominant thrust of recent proposals seems to be development of new programs or extension of existing programs that are essentially similar to those now in place. Little attention is given to possible ways of extensively restructuring the logic and approach of existing programs or to rethinking the fundamentals of approaches that have evolved.

In view of current issues and likely future developments, rethinking some of the fundamentals of policies affecting the elderly seems particularly relevant. This chapter sketches some ideas that should be considered.

Resources of the Elderly

One of the basic starting points for this discussion involves the resources available to the elderly. On average, incomes of the elderly

TABLE 5-1

SHARES OF MONEY INCOME BY SOURCE FOR AGED FAMILIES, 1984

(percent)

Source of Income	Individuals 65 or Older Living Alone or with Nonrelatives Only	Families with Householder 65 or Older
Earnings	7	29
Public program payments		
Social security	43	32
Supplemental Security Income	2	1
Other programs	2	1
Other sources		
Dividends, interest, rent	33	24
Employment-related		
pensions, alimony, annuities	13	14
Total percent	100	100
Median income (dollars)	7,527	18,257

SOURCE: *Social Security Bulletin,* Annual Statistical Supplement, 1986, table 9, p. 75.

are reasonably adequate, and many elderly people have significant assets. The economic status of the elderly compared with the rest of the population has improved. The ratio of incomes of elderly families to incomes of nonelderly families increased from 0.59 in 1970 to 0.69 in 1983, largely because of disproportionate increases in social security payments. Between 1970 and 1983, for example, the average monthly social security benefit for retired workers increased by 273 percent, compared with a 138 percent increase in median annual wages and salaries.

In addition, the elderly do not generally need to rely exclusively on social security payments. Many have significant assets, as shown in John Weicher's chapter. For the elderly as a group, social security benefits account for well below half their money income as shown in table 5-1. Some of the elderly, however, have low incomes. This discussion also assumes that public support will be made available for those whose incomes are grossly inadequate, although the levels of support and the conditions under which it is made available will remain controversial.

These propositions are an important starting point for discussion because the general approach I propose to examine includes an expanded role for individual choice. And individual choice presupposes the available resources allowing such choices.

Framework for Rethinking Policies and Programs

The overall effectiveness of government policies should be evaluated in terms of two broad considerations. One is whether the policies help direct available resources to their most highly valued uses. In economic terms, this is a supply-side question. The other is whether the policies induce citizens as consumers to choose among goods and services that reflect their preferences, given their financial resources and available supplementary resources. This is a demand-side question. The incentives that influence decisions affect both sides of the equation and are affected by program structure.

Government programs and policies are, of course, intended to produce outcomes that differ from conditions that would prevail in their absence. The design and administration of programs and policies, however, involve incentives that face both public and private decision makers. Consequently, actual outcomes reflect these incentives, and resources are usually not mobilized as effectively as possible to satisfy the preferences of citizens.

The incentives that influence public and private choices are affected by factors such as whether costs are explicit, whose budget is affected, and how payment takes place. Examples are varied and complex, but too little attention to implications for real resource usage is a common result.

When costs and their incidence are not apparent, their effects on resource usage are often not adequately taken into account. For consumers, the costs of trade protection are obscure, for example, while the benefits to those protected are usually evident. The costs of rent control due to scarcity of rental units, poor maintenance, and malallocation of available units are less explicit than the difference between controlled and market rental rates.

Regarding budgets, politicians are often attracted to off-budget instead of on-budget spending. Much regulation, such as antipollution requirements, places costs on the budgets of businesses instead of government. Before the introduction of the volunteer armed forces, for example, a large share of the costs was placed on the "budgets" of the conscripts themselves instead of on the federal budget. This approach is also evident in recent legislation that requires privately provided health plans to cover former employees and in proposals that mandate employers to finance health coverage for all workers.

71

Farm programs illustrate the importance of the way in which payment takes place. We have grown used to farm subsidies in the form of commodities payments so large that they would surely be scandalous if they were simply paid in cash. When cost reimbursement forms the basis for payments, it becomes necessary to regulate conditions for reimbursement. Regulations are typically developed that specify in detail the kinds of services that qualify, the credentials of providers, and usually—to contain costs—limits on prices and amounts of services as well.

The health care system has always relied extensively on cost reimbursement as the basis for payments, and government has increasingly assumed the role of third-party payer. To contain costs, limits have frequently been placed on rates and entry, an approach that relies on regulation rather than competition to produce and allocate health care services. Efforts to hold down costs have often taken the form of reducing allowable fees and charges that are reimbursed by Medicare and Medicaid. These policies are presumably intended to force doctors and hospitals to absorb some of the costs instead of shifting them to patients by, for example, requiring more cost sharing through deductibles or coinsurance. This approach raises the question of whether health care consumers gain at the expense of doctors and hospitals, or whether instead the amounts of services are arbitrarily reduced and the kinds of services reshuffled. In any case, the main goal is usually containing budgetary costs. Whether such cost containment policies reduce consumer benefits more than real resource use usually gets far less attention.

The structure and design of many programs lead to a focus on factors other than real resource costs. For example, when military enlisted men were paid less than market wages, decisions on personnel use were made primarily on the basis of budget costs instead of real resource costs. Regulations formulated as standards that private firms or other units of government must meet have frequently been criticized because they pay too little attention to the magnitude of real resource costs. Because the costs of trade protection are not explicit, consumers usually pay little attention to the increased real resource use necessary to produce substitutes domestically. Similarly, a substantial share of farm subsidy payments is dissipated through higher expenditures for such items as equipment and fertilizers, increasing what society pays to support farm incomes. These examples illustrate inadequate attention to implications for real resource use when policies are designed.

The goal of economic activity generally, and of policies influencing it, should be to obtain the highest output of goods and services that can be produced by the real resources available. This idea can be stated equivalently as minimizing real resource costs necessary to achieve any given level of output of goods and services. Because in many areas of public policy the main focus is on current government budgets, implications for resource use frequently receive insufficient attention. This may be particularly important for the elderly because the federal government has assumed a growing responsibility to provide them with income support and health care services.

Work and Aging

Tax treatment of the earnings of social security recipients provides a straightforward example of a policy that creates adverse incentives from the standpoint of effective resource use. Retired social security recipients lose 50 cents in benefits for every additional dollar they earn above $8,400 per year up to the age of seventy. (This amount is scheduled to decline to 33⅓ cents beginning in 1990.) The income from social security payments that must be given up as earnings rise is equivalent to a tax of 50 percent that is imposed in addition to normal personal income taxes. Like other taxes on income, this implicit tax is a disincentive to work. The number of working hours at which the disincentive begins is lower for people who earn higher hourly wages, and who, by that measure, have the most valuable output to contribute.

Although this policy is ostensibly intended to keep down social security outlays, it also has the presumably unintended effect of reducing work. The policy thus wastes resources that otherwise would contribute to society. This discouraging effect on work is particularly ironic in view of the desirability of encouraging the sense of personal worth gained by the elderly through contributing constructively to society. A significant fraction of people over sixty-five work at least some time during the year, as shown in table 5–2. The fraction declines with advancing age, particularly for year-round full-time work. More than one-third of men between sixty-five and sixty-nine, the age group to which the earnings test applies, worked in 1985. Only a small share of these, of course, is affected by the earnings test.

Taxes inevitably produce some resource waste as a byproduct. Clearly, however, reducing the unusually high (implicit plus explicit) marginal tax rates applicable to social security recipients (within the age and earnings range involved) would avoid unnecessary waste. The evidence from recent research indicates that raising or abandoning the earnings test would have only a small effect on social security

73

TABLE 5–2
WORK EXPERIENCE OF PERSONS AGED SIXTY-FIVE AND OLDER, 1985
(percent)

Ages	Worked in 1985	Year Round		Part Year	
		Full time	Part time	Full time	Part time
Both sexes 65 and older	15.1	4.3	3.7	2.4	4.6
Men 65 and older	22.7	7.4	4.8	3.9	6.6
65–69	35.3	13.6	6.2	6.7	8.9
70–74	21.3	5.0	5.6	3.3	7.4
75–79	11.9	3.2	3.0	1.7	4.0
80 and older	7.7	1.9	2.4	0.9	2.5
Women 65 and older	9.7	2.2	2.9	1.4	3.2
65–69	18.4	4.8	4.8	3.2	5.6
70–74	8.9	1.4	3.1	1.0	3.4
75–79	4.9	0.9	1.8	0.4	1.8
80 and older	2.1	0.3	0.9	0.2	0.7

SOURCE: Bureau of Labor Statistics, March 1986, Current Population Survey public use tapes.

recipients' work behavior, mainly because few people would be affected. Correspondingly, of course, there would only be a small increase in budget outlays. The focus of policy attention should be shifted, however, from budget outlays to implications for the use of human resources. Tax and benefit policies should be adapted as necessary to prevent discouraging the elderly from working and earning money.

The fact that older workers are subject to federal minimum wage requirements is also ironic in view of social goals for the elderly. To benefit as a society from the experience and capabilities of retired workers, as well as to enhance retirees' personal satisfaction, older people are frequently encouraged to volunteer for worthwhile activities. Although they are encouraged to work at a zero wage, however, older workers are precluded from working for below minimum wages. It would seem that some additional older workers might be encouraged to use their talents and skills if they received low wages instead of none at all. Some might benefit from the income earned at low wages by at least covering possible out-of-pocket expenses. Again, there should be more emphasis on using human resources effectively and less on artificial and—for the elderly—irrelevant constructs like whether full-time work at a certain wage would support a family of four at the poverty level.

Health and Aging

Programs to support health care generally have been designed to reimburse costs incurred, both for the population as a whole and for the elderly. Reimbursement policies are tempered, of course, by delineating what is covered by plans and by deductible and copayment provisions. For many acute health problems, the cost-reimbursement structure of health plans may entail providing few services other than those the patient would choose to pay for in a more market-oriented context. Higher deductibles and copayments apparently reduce the amount of services demanded, however. The costs of providing the services might also be lower if competition replaced cost reimbursement.

For some aspects of health care, even in instances of acute health problems, individual choice might be given a larger role. When the health services include a substantial rehabilitation element, for example, it might be reasonable to emphasize support from family or friends outside an institutional framework. Self-help activities, homespun remedies, or extensive reliance on family and home support are clearly inadequate for many health problems. Yet their role has probably been artificially diminished by the historical emphasis on cost reimbursement to formal institutions providing health care. Shifting the structure and emphasis of health plans toward payments based on the medical conditions of people experiencing health problems might encourage the provision of more services outside institutions.

The introduction of payments based on diagnosis-related group (DRG) formulas can be viewed as a step toward reimbursement based on the patient's problem and condition instead of on the tabulation of actual resource costs. This prospective payment system, whether based on costs for the institution providing health care services or on average costs for all hospitals, amounts to an alternative formula for computing costs to be reimbursed—an alternative to simply computing estimated costs for each patient.

How such alternative formulas could help control overall costs is not entirely clear, but the concept is interesting. If it were applied beyond the institutional setting, prospective payment could lead to a better voluntarily chosen balance between services provided by institutions and those provided in other ways.

Application to Long-Term Care

For the elderly, it is particularly interesting to consider the application of payment systems that are alternatives to those based on cost-reimbursement concepts for long-term care, such as that often provided in nursing homes. Such alternatives could potentially both increase the quality of services and economize on use of resources. The key element in such an alternative concept would be payments based on well-defined descriptions of health status, capabilities, and disabilities of the individual instead of on the costs of treatment that qualify for reimbursement.

Payments based on individual health status and condition are not entirely alien to our system of social programs. A recent demonstration project sponsored by the U.S. Department of Health and Human Services used somewhat similar principles. The channeling approach in this long-term-care project provided detailed management of community care resources to support the elderly in their homes instead of in nursing homes. The project evaluation showed "improved satisfaction with life for clients and the informal care givers who bear most of the care burden." Although budget costs were apparently somewhat higher under this approach, whether total real costs were higher is unclear. The effects on informal care givers suggest that total costs might be significantly lower.

Other programs have used cash payment approaches more directly. Payments under our workers' compensation program, for example, derive from analysis and assessment of the value of a worker's impairment. The formulas may be crude and subject to criticism and refinement. But the merit of this approach is that payments are made without the need to demonstrate that corresponding real resource costs have been incurred. Disability payments are also calculated according to degrees of impairment instead of on cost-reimbursement formulas.

It must be recognized, of course, that formulas for workers' compensation and disability payments arose from a logic entirely different from that for health care payments. There is no reason in principle, however, why the underlying concept that has been used for the workplace could not be applied to the health care arena. Disability payments have been figured on estimates of actual loss in earning power. Health care payments could be based on estimates of the loss in spending power caused by the costs of ill health or incapacitation. That is, payment schedules could be set to cover some fraction of the additional costs that would need to be incurred to compensate for the effects of ill health or incapacity in ordinary daily life.

Consider how payment concepts structured along these lines might be applied to elderly people with chronic long-term health problems and partial disabilities. The application could be similar whether payments were financed by private insurance or by Medicaid, which now contributes importantly to financing nursing home care. Benefits under both private insurance plans and Medicaid are now tied to institutions providing care instead of to the functional status of the recipient. Under the approach proposed here, payment eligibility would depend on the person's health and disability instead of on cost reimbursement. Moreover, in contrast to voucher concepts, cash payments would be made and the money could be dispensed as the person affected (or legal guardian) saw fit. That is, payment would not be contingent on obtaining specified services from a qualified or certified provider. Informal or family-supported arrangements could be made at the discretion of those affected.

The most significant potential advantage of a program structured in this way would be resource savings. Cost-reimbursement approaches create unrelenting pressures to devote increasing amounts of resources to programs because, as long as recipients enjoy any benefit, they desire expansion even if the additional resource commitments are large relative to the benefits. Moreover, the present system has an all-or-nothing character. People must initially finance

77

their own care almost entirely until they are pauperized. They can then qualify to obtain public assistance that may be far costlier to provide than if some financial support had been available earlier.

Pressures for expansion under a cash payment structure might also be less severe because many recipients could realize greater real benefits. Elderly people are typically extremely reluctant to move into nursing homes, even if they are severely incapacitated. For their relatives and friends, institutional care may be the only realistic alternative if there is no other available support from outside sources, such as Medicaid. If eligibility and payment levels were based on the elderly person's functional condition, a wider range of options might be feasible. For example, part-time paid care and voluntary assistance from family and friends might be arranged. The recipients of such care might see themselves as better off in terms of the real benefits they receive, even though resource costs might be lower than under a cost-reimbursement-based institutional alternative.

The burden on family members or friends of providing care for the elderly would be significantly alleviated if they were compensated and could supplement their own efforts with paid assistants. A variety of informal arrangements could be made, consistent with the diversity of actual real-world circumstances. Such arrangements could supplement the incomes of those who were compensated for providing care and in addition provide a sense of personal satisfaction from such work. With the projected increase in two-generation geriatric families, the younger but retired generation could significantly contribute to providing both services and valuable social and family contact.

Provision of benefits in the form of cash payments might be criticized because of concerns about quality control. Situations in which the elderly are abused also occur under the current system, however. The main problems arise with those elderly whose mental competence is failing and who lack a responsible guardian or a concerned informal support network. In the absence of these conditions, however, it seems preferable to suppose that these elderly, as well as their family and friends, can best judge whether care is adequate. Certainly, they have the most direct interest.

For institutional care or other services delivered on a cost-reimbursed basis, conditions under which care is provided and the credentials of the providers are typically highly regulated. These regulations are generally based on a medical services model that specifies, for example, what services should be provided by a registered nurse and when physician supervision or visits are required. For elderly with partial disabilities, good quality services may depend more on the caring, concern, and reliability of the provider than on professional health service credentials. The most essential need for many among the elderly may be regular daily or periodic checking to see how the person is doing instead of professional medical attention. Overreliance on a medical model and on credentialization stimulated partly by a need to ensure integrity in a cost-reimbursement system tends to drive up costs excessively. Moreover, in many instances following the medical model leads to the wrong pattern of care from the viewpoint of the elderly person because it fails to meet his or her real needs.

Another question is whether a cash payment system might reduce volunteer work or community support systems. Care giving on a fully voluntary basis might be reduced if some compensation were made available. Voluntary efforts should, of course, continue to be encouraged by persuasion. The main virtue of the cash payment system is that exhortation could be supplemented by incentives. Moreover, providing some compensation to someone who was previously a volunteer does not by itself mean devoting more resources to care giving. In considering whether purely voluntary efforts might be somewhat diminished, it is critical to determine whether the services that are provided meet real needs more effectively and whether these needs are being met with lower resource costs. The goal is optimal use of real resources, not minimization of monetary costs or compensation.

A cash payment system contingent on physical condition might help facilitate expansion of private insurance coverage for long-term care of the elderly. Many elderly might choose to purchase private insurance to guard against pauperization in the event of health or impairment problems. Unless such an approach were publicly subsidized, it would not entail cross-subsidization between groups. But it would accomplish risk spreading. Uncertainties about how individual choices, and hence reimbursable costs, might be affected by private insurance coverage are often regarded as one reason why such insurance is very costly and has played only a very limited role. If eligibility for benefits and payment levels were both based on an assessment of physical health conditions and degree of impairment, however, uncertainties due to choices among services with very different resource costs would be eliminated, thus lowering private insurance premiums.

Under a cash payment system based on assessment of the individual's health condition, institutional long-term care would still play a significant role. Decisions by the health-impaired elderly about whether to use it, however, would be based on their assessment of

79

whether this would be the best arrangement under the circumstances instead of on whether institutional care would give them access to public or insurance-provided resources. The financial costs of a program structured in this way would not necessarily be lower. But the real resource costs would surely be lower than under a system in which payment levels are supported only by demonstrations of actual resource use.

Conclusions

The central point of this discussion is that, in the formulation of public policy, greater attention should be focused on implications for real resource use. Programs should be structured to economize on total use of resources and to use available resources as effectively as possible. Programs like social security should be structured to encourage work choices for elderly people who can and would work if they did not have to overcome severe incentive penalties. At a minimum, such programs should avoid discouraging work any more than is inevitable under the general tax system.

For the elderly who need services like long-term health care, programs should be structured to economize on overall real resource use and to make the most effective use possible of resources that could contribute to personal care. Programs based on cost-reimbursement, where payments are channeled primarily through institutional providers, are inimical to both objectives. These programs should be restructured to enable people to profit financially from choices among alternatives and to obtain the larger nonmonetary benefits that may be possible through more diverse and often informal arrangements.

Implementing the concepts outlined here is surely more difficult than stating the basic principles that should be applied. Detailed analysis of how existing programs operate and how they would need to be modified to incorporate these principles is a formidable task. Keeping implications for real resource use the central concern of analysis is essential. Enlarging the role of individual choices to facilitate the achievement of preferred arrangements for services provided while economizing on real resource costs is equally important. If we bear these principles in mind, it should be possible to design approaches superior to those we are now pursuing.

6
The Increase in Early Retirement since 1969

Wayne Vroman and Susan Vroman

Early retirement is becoming increasingly common in the United States. Early exits from the labor force are occurring despite increases in the average life expectancy of the population. Combined, these two developments mean that our older population will spend more years in retirement than earlier generations of older Americans. And if recent trends in early retirement and life expectancy continue, the elderly will experience even longer periods in retirement in future years.

These developments have several implications, the most obvious and perhaps most important being their short-run effects on the social security (or Old-Age, Survivors, Disability, and Health Insurance—OASDHI) trust funds. OASDHI contributions are reduced when workers retire at increasingly younger ages, and outlays are increased by the combined effects of early retirement and increased longevity. It can be argued that for a given amount of outlays social security and other retirement benefits are better targeted when a higher proportion of payments is made to the older segment of the eligible population while those of younger ages continue to work.

The increase in early retirement may reflect a response to institutional constraints and financial incentives. Recent federal legislation has tried to encourage later retirement and to permit more part-time work by the elderly. The age of mandatory retirement was increased from sixty-five to seventy by the 1978 amendments to the Age Discrimination in Employment Act. The Social Security Amendments of 1983 included a provision to raise the age of eligibility for full OASDHI retirement benefits from the present sixty-five to sixty-six in the year 2009 and to sixty-seven in 2027.[1] The combined OASDHI and federal, state, or local civil service retirement benefits for new beneficiaries were reduced by a pension offset provision included in the 1983 Social Security Amendments, which was aimed at reducing perceived inequities due to "double dipping." Future retirees subject to this provision will receive smaller OASDHI monthly payments.

This legislation also made social security benefits partially taxable under the federal personal income tax and provided higher benefits for those who keep working past age sixty-five (a larger delayed retirement credit). The earnings test for OASDHI beneficiaries has been substantially liberalized since the early 1970s to permit increased annual hours of work and earnings, and the maximum age of its applicability was reduced from seventy-one to sixty-nine in 1983. All these changes provide incentives for increased work by older persons.

Despite these legislative changes, it is not at all obvious that the labor supply of the elderly will increase. A powerful trend toward reduced labor supply among the elderly has existed throughout the twentieth century.[2] During the 1970s and 1980s the pace of labor supply reductions in some age groups appears to have accelerated. In the face of generally weak growth in aggregate demand, numerous and severe recessions, and an influx of younger persons into the labor force, early retirement and disability retirement in the public and private sectors have grown rapidly. The forces causing reductions of labor supply among older workers may not be stemmed by the recent legislation.

This paper examines the earlier exit of older workers from the labor force and investigates possible explanations for this major labor market change. The primary focus is on early retirement. Much work has already been done that analyzes the labor force participation of workers over sixty-five, but the sharp decline in participation of workers fifty-five to sixty-four has received less attention. The paper singles out one aspect of declining labor supply: the growing importance of complete withdrawal from the labor force by men in this age group. The proportion of these men who report they do no work at all during the year has grown, particularly since 1969.

The paper is divided into five sections. The first discusses in more detail the decline in the labor supply of the elderly. The second examines several possible explanations for this phenomenon. The third and fourth focus on two factors, declining health and increased availability of transfer payments, that may account for it. The last section contains some brief concluding remarks.

The paper is a descriptive analysis. It relies heavily on tabulations of data from two large-scale microdata bases, the Current Population Survey (CPS) of the U.S. Census Bureau and the National Health Interview Survey (HIS) of the U.S. Department of Health and Human Services. Tabulations of both data bases were conducted at the Urban Institute. Using tabulations of microdata, it is hoped, will enable the paper to reach a wider audience than relying primarily on regressions and other more sophisticated analytic techniques.

After documenting the recent labor supply reductions, the paper reaches two main conclusions. First, despite survey responses that seem to suggest the opposite, the average health of the elderly has not deteriorated in recent years. Second, the increased availability of income support payments (disability and retirement transfers) has contributed to the increased prevalence of early retirement.

The Declining Labor Supply of the Elderly

Large-scale reductions in the labor supply of older workers are apparent in several kinds of time series data. Labor force participation rates, the most commonly used indicators of labor supply, provide useful summary measures of the size of the reductions. During the thirty years from 1954 to 1984, labor force participation rates declined for all age groups of older men.[3] The absolute decline was largest for those sixty-five and older, from 40.5 percent to 16.3 percent, or 24.2 percentage points. Nearly as large, however, was the decline among men fifty-five to sixty-four, from 88.7 percent to 68.5 percent, or 20.2 percentage points. Even among men forty-five to fifty-four the participation rate declined more than 5 percentage points, from 96.5 percent in 1954 to 91.2 percent in 1984.

The trend toward declining labor supply among older men appears to have accelerated in the 1970s and 1980s. For workers forty-five to sixty-four the pace of the labor supply reductions has been faster since 1970 than from 1954 to 1969.

Because of the increased labor force participation of women since the 1950s, the association between increased retirement and reduced labor force participation rates is less obvious. Between 1954 and 1984 the participation rate for women over sixty-five declined 1.8 percentage points (from 9.3 percent to 7.5 percent) while that for women fifty-five to sixty-four increased 11.6 percentage points (from 30.1 percent to 41.7 percent). This, however, should be compared with the 19.0-percentage-point increase in the participation rate for all women sixteen and older. When the labor force participation rates for older women are compared with those for younger women, it is clear that the labor supply of older women has grown more slowly. Only among women sixty-five and older has there been a decline in the participation rate, and that decline was very small. Because of the difficulty of disentangling the change in retirement behavior of older women from the general increase in women's labor force attachment, the rest of this paper focuses on older men, since they account for most of the increased retirement and particularly the increase in early retirement.

Reductions in labor supply can take several forms. People may decide to work fewer weeks per year or to stop working altogether. Both actions cause labor force participation rates to decline. What is interesting about the recent reductions of labor supply among older men is that so much of the change reflects decisions to stop work altogether.

In March of each year the monthly labor force survey of households (the CPS) includes supplemental questions that focus on labor force activities during the entire previous calendar year.[4] Table 6-1 summarizes the responses to some of these questions. Among men twenty-five and older the proportion who did not work at all during the year nearly doubled between 1954 and 1984, from 11.1 percent in 1954 to 21.5 percent in 1984.

Increases in the proportion not working occurred in all age groups, even those twenty-five to thirty-four and thirty-five to forty-four, but the increases were larger for older groups. Clearly a large segment of the male population does not wait until sixty-five to leave the labor force. Much of the reduction in labor supply that has occurred among men fifty-five to sixty-four has taken the form of complete withdrawal from the labor force.

Growth in the proportions of older men not working is also shown in data for social security (or OASDHI) beneficiaries. Beneficiaries are subject to a retirement test, which limits the amount of covered earnings that can be received without a loss of benefits. The provisions of the retirement test have undergone many changes. The annual earnings allowed without a reduction in annual social security benefits increased from $1,200 in 1955 to $7,320 in 1985.[5]

One of the authors has conducted two analyses of the retirement test, the first covering the years 1962–1967 and the second the years 1970–1980.[6] Table 6-2 presents data from the second study that summarize the earnings of male beneficiaries aged sixty-five to seventy-one.

Among social security beneficiaries sixty-five to seventy-one the proportion not working was much higher in 1980 than in 1970, and a much smaller proportion had earnings close to the annual exempt amount. For the 1970–1980 period the labor supply of beneficiaries sixty-five to seventy-one decreased by more than half.[7] During the 1970s an increased proportion of male beneficiaries decided to stop working altogether, and labor supply clearly declined. This happened despite changes in the retirement test that made it possible for

TABLE 6–1
MALE POPULATION NOT WORKING DURING THE YEAR,
BY AGE GROUP, 1954–1984
(percent)

	25–34	35–44	45–54	55–59	60–64	65–69	70 and Older	25 and Older
1954	2.2	1.6	2.4	6.7	13.7	33.1	68.0	11.1
1959	2.8	2.3	3.7	7.4	14.6	39.2	69.3	12.3
1964	2.2	2.1	3.4	7.1	15.9	42.7	74.3	13.8
1969	2.2	2.0	4.0	8.2	16.4	42.3	74.4	13.9
1974	3.3	3.5	6.7	12.4	21.7	55.4	77.5	16.8
1979	4.0	3.9	7.2	15.4	29.5	61.6	82.1	19.0
1984	5.8	5.9	9.3	18.1	35.8	67.1	84.9	21.5
Change 1954–84 (percentage points)	3.6	4.3	6.9	11.4	22.1	34.0	16.9	10.4

SOURCE: Based on tabulations of the Current Population Survey. Data for 1954 to 1974 from U.S. Department of Labor, *Work Experience of the Population*, various issues. Data for 1979 and 1984 from unpublished U.S. Department of Labor tabulations.

TABLE 6–2

EARNINGS OF MALE OASDHI RETIREMENT BENEFICIARIES
AGED SIXTY-FIVE THROUGH SEVENTY-ONE, 1970 AND 1980
(percent)

	Zero	Below Exempt Amount[a]	Near Exempt Amount[b]	Above Exempt Amount[c]
1970	58.7	16.6	7.9	16.9
1980	78.9	15.9	1.4	3.7

a. Less than $1,501 in 1970 and $4,901 in 1980.
b. Between $1,501 and $1,800 in 1970 and $4,901 and $5,100 in 1980.
c. More than $1,800 in 1970 and $5,100 in 1980.
SOURCES: Based on unpublished tabulations of the March 1978 CPS Summary Earnings Record exact match file done at the Urban Institute. See Vroman, "Some Economic Effects."

beneficiaries to increase their labor supply without losing benefits. For the two years 1970 and 1980 a worker earning the average hourly earnings for the economy would have been able to work 520 and 751 hours, respectively, without losing benefits. That is, the permissible number of annual hours rose 44 percent between 1970 and 1980.

What is responsible for the increase in the proportion of older men who do not work at all during the year? The March work experience survey conducted by the U.S. Labor Department has asked this question for several years. Table 6–3 shows that the proportions of men who did not work because of retirement increased in all four age groups. Retirement is now the most important stated reason for not working among men sixty to sixty-four as well as among men sixty-five and older. Among men forty-five to fifty-four and fifty-five to fifty-nine, being ill or disabled is the most important stated reason for not working. There were measurable increases in the proportions not working for health reasons, particularly between 1969 and 1979. Among men of early retirement ages, that is, fifty-five to fifty-nine and sixty to sixty-four, the 1979–1984 period saw a sharp increase in the proportion who were retired and a decline in the proportion who reported themselves ill or disabled. By 1984 nearly one man in four aged sixty to sixty-four reported not working because of retirement. Even at ages fifty-five to fifty-nine men are increasingly giving retirement as their reason for not working. In 1984 roughly one man in ten fifty-five to sixty-four reported not working because of illness or disability. The reasons why older men do not work are examined in more detail in subsequent sections.

TABLE 6-3
REASONS GIVEN BY OLDER MEN FOR NOT WORKING, BY AGE GROUP, 1969–1984
(percent)

	All Reasons	Ill or Disabled	Retired	Unemployed	All Other Reasons
45–54					
1969	4.0	3.2	0.4	0.1	0.3
1974	6.7	5.4	0.5	0.5	0.4
1979	7.2	5.5	0.8	0.4	0.5
1984	9.3	5.6	1.1	1.6	1.0
Change, 1969–84 (percentage points)	5.3	2.4	0.7	1.5	0.7
55–59					
1969	8.2	6.4	1.4	0.1	0.2
1974	12.4	8.8	2.7	0.7	0.1
1979	15.4	9.9	4.4	0.3	0.9
1984	18.1	9.3	6.5	1.6	0.8
Change, 1969–84 (percentage points)	9.9	2.9	5.1	1.5	0.6
60–64					
1969	16.4	8.5	7.3	0.3	0.3
1974	21.7	12.0	9.0	0.4	0.3
1979	29.5	14.8	13.9	0.2	0.6
1984	35.8	10.4	24.2	0.5	0.7
Change, 1969–84 (percentage points)	19.4	1.9	16.9	0.2	0.4
65 and older					
1969	62.2	13.6	47.7	0.3	0.5
1974	68.7	14.7	53.3	0.5	0.3
1979	74.1	13.1	59.8	0.3	0.8
1984	78.2	9.6	67.6	0.3	0.7
Change, 1969–84 (percentage points)	16.0	4.0	19.9	0.0	0.2

NOTE: The totals may not add to the sum in the "All Reasons" column because of rounding.
SOURCE: Based on tabulations of the Current Population Survey. Data for 1969 and 1974 from U.S. Department of Labor, *Work Experience of the Population*. Data for 1979 and 1984 from unpublished U.S. Department of Labor tabulations.

In sum, since 1954 the labor supply of all male groups forty-five and older has been measurably reduced. The reduction occurred more rapidly between 1969 and 1984 than between 1954 and 1969. Much of the reduction has taken the form of sharply increased proportions of older men who do not work at all during the year. Reductions are observed among OASDHI beneficiaries as well as other groups in the older male population. When asked why they do not work, men usually give retirement or disability as the reason.

Possible Explanations

In examining possible explanations for the observed reductions of labor supply among older men, it is useful to differentiate between the two components of the change: earlier retirement (that is, complete withdrawal from the labor force); and a reduction in hours worked by older men who continue to participate in the work force. This distinction is intended not to deny that the two are interconnected but to simplify the analysis. Certainly, part-time or part-year employment for several years may be a substitute for earlier retirement; it cushions the reduction in retirement income that would be implied by earlier retirement. Nonetheless, we feel that more can be gained by simplifying the discussion and treating the two aspects of reduced labor supply separately. Our discussion centers on early retirement, which has the greater effect on labor supply.

Earlier Retirement. A wide range of factors influence a worker's decision to retire. Two noneconomic factors may have contributed to the increase in early retirement. One of these is a change in social attitudes; that is, the age at which it is customary or socially acceptable to retire may have declined. In addition, changes in health may have influenced retirement. The next section discusses the possibility that deteriorating health has contributed to the increase in early retirement.

Several economic factors must also be considered in explaining the increase. One possible contributory factor may be a decline in the demand for labor. In other words, the change may have been generated from the demand side of the labor market, with supply simply responding. Demand for older workers may have declined for several reasons. First, weak macroeconomic performance has led to a reduction in the demand for labor over the past fifteen years. Since 1973 the economy has been operating with higher unemployment rates, and laid-off older workers are more likely to retire because it is difficult for them to find new jobs in a weak macroeconomic environment. This is particularly true in industries where demand is declining secularly, for example, because of international competition. Displaced older workers are generally less able than younger workers to make the transition to new industries that require different skills or relocation. In addition to macroeconomic reasons for reduced demand, individual firms with an interest in cutting costs may encourage older workers to retire earlier so as to replace them with younger workers who earn lower wages.

A final set of explanations arises from the microeconomic analysis of lifetime labor supply. If a person's utility depends on leisure (taken after retirement) and the present value of lifetime income (a proxy for the consumption of goods purchased with the income), economic theory predicts that, other things being equal, the person would choose to retire when the benefit of working another year (the added retirement and current income) does not compensate for the lost year's leisure.[8] To derive this result analytically along with the associated comparative statics results requires a formal model. On the basis of a simple formal model of lifetime labor supply,[9] earlier retirement could be caused by an increase in retirement benefits, a decrease in preretirement salary,[10] or a decline in life expectancy (which has not occurred). The fourth section of this paper discusses the effect of changes in retirement income on older men's labor supply.

Reduced Hours. The older worker's choice of labor hours can be analyzed by use of the standard labor supply model. This model hypothesizes that a person maximizes utility, which depends on annual leisure hours and annual income, subject to a budget constraint (annual income = nonlabor income + labor income). From such an analysis certain standard results arise. First, an increase in unearned income leads to a reduction in labor supply, because leisure is a normal good, that is, demand for leisure increases with income. An increase in a person's market wage has an ambiguous effect on the person's labor supply. On the one hand, an increase in the hourly wage raises the opportunity cost of an hour of leisure and thus leads to an increase in labor supply (the substitution effect); on the other hand, it raises income for any given labor supply, which leads to a reduction in labor supply (the income effect). Thus the effect of a change in the wage on the person's labor supply will depend on which effect is stronger—the substitution or the income effect.

In describing the labor supply of older workers, this model needs to be amended slightly. Workers sixty-two to sixty-nine who are eligible for social security face a somewhat more complex budget

89

constraint because of the social security retirement test. Briefly, full benefits are received by workers who earn less than the exempt amount, which in 1985 was $5,400 for those under sixty-five and $7,320 for those sixty-five to sixty-nine. Benefits are reduced fifty cents for each dollar earned above the exempt amount. Thus up to the exempt amount social security constitutes an increase in nonlabor income (a disincentive to labor supply). Beyond the exempt amount (until benefits are reduced to zero), social security lowers the effective wage rate by 50 percent. Standard theory predicts that such a system will lead to a reduction in hours worked by recipients.

Health Status

Decreased labor force participation among older men might reflect a worsening of their health. The effect of poor health on labor supply has been examined by several researchers, but no consensus has been reached.[11] This section presents information on the health of all male age groups sixteen and older. Presenting details for the entire age distribution places the experiences of older men in a broader context that may reflect underlying health trends in the male population. The experiences of men fifty-five to sixty-four will be of most interest since they have shown such large recent reductions in labor supply.

The starting point is a discussion of data from the National Health Interview Survey on self-reported health, as summarized in table 6–4.[12] Since 1972 respondents have been asked to assess their own health in relation to that of other men of the same age, with responses falling into four categories: excellent, good, fair, and poor. Although the question is designed to elicit information on relative health, the responses appear to be assessments of absolute health— the proportion reporting poor health rises as the age of the group rises.

Between 1972 and 1980 self-assessments of health were practically unchanged in all male age groups. The largest change was the 2.5-percentage-point increase among men sixty to sixty-four reporting poor health. The final column of the table shows an ordinal index of health status, which assigns weights of 4, 3, 2, and 1 to persons reporting excellent, good, fair, and poor health, respectively. We have not conducted formal statistical tests of the significance of these changes, but it is clear that the self-reported health of men fifty-five to sixty-four did not undergo any unusual deterioration between 1972 and 1980. The predominant impression conveyed by these data is one of stable health during the 1970s.

Whatever may be true of recent trends in average health, there

TABLE 6-4

SELF-REPORTED HEALTH STATUS OF THE MALE POPULATION, BY AGE GROUP, 1972 AND 1980

	Percentage in Poor Health[a]			Percentage in Good Health[a,b]			Ordinal Index of Average Health Status[c]		
	1972	1980	Change	1972	1980	Change	1972	1980	Change
16–19	0.6	0.3	−0.3	95.5	95.5	0.0	3.548	3.556	0.008
20–24	0.8	0.8	0.0	94.1	93.8	−0.3	3.527	3.503	−0.024
25–34	1.0	1.2	0.2	94.0	93.4	−0.6	3.562	3.507	−0.055
35–44	2.1	2.6	0.5	90.7	89.8	−0.9	3.448	3.412	−0.036
45–54	4.2	4.5	0.3	83.5	83.7	0.2	3.242	3.237	−0.005
55–59	7.8	7.4	−0.4	75.3	76.3	1.0	3.039	3.079	0.040
60–64	7.7	10.2	2.5	71.8	72.5	0.7	2.965	2.951	−0.014
65–69	8.9	10.5	1.6	69.1	67.5	−1.6	2.919	2.860	−0.059
70+	9.7	8.7	−1.0	68.7	68.2	−0.5	2.906	2.902	−0.004
16+	3.6	3.7	0.1	86.1	86.1	0.0	3.330	3.321	−0.009
16+, fixed age weights[d]	3.5	3.7	0.2	86.4	86.1	−0.3	3.340	3.321	−0.019

a. Responses to a question in which people were asked to rate their health in relation to that of other persons of the same age.
b. Persons reporting that they were in good health or in excellent health.
c. An index in which excellent health was scaled at 4, good health at 3, fair health at 2, and poor health at 1.
d. 1980 age weights were used to reweight the 1972 data.
SOURCE: Based on tabulations of the Health Interview Survey conducted at the Urban Institute.

seems little doubt that people are becoming more conscious of their health and are making greater efforts to improve it. In recent years they have increasingly tried to improve their physical fitness through a combination of increased exercise and changes in eating, drinking, and smoking habits. These changes may be partly responsible for the declining death rates.

To throw further light on this issue, table 6–5 displays data on objective measures of health: death rates, visits to doctors, and hospital days. Death rates declined at all ages. This trend, which has affected all adult groups of men and women, dates from the late 1960s and early 1970s.[13] Between 1972 and 1980 death rates declined about 20 percent in all age groups from thirty-five to sixty-four. Smaller percentage reductions took place in the two oldest groups. Overall, male death rates declined about 15 percent.

Per capita visits to doctors and hospital days as reported in the HIS also declined between 1972 and 1980. Decreases were registered in eight of the nine age groups for both measures. Only among men fifty-five to fifty-nine was there a small increase in visits to doctors. These decreases merit some additional comments.

To understand what these data imply about the health of older workers, consider the following model of the market for visits to doctors. (A similar model could be constructed for hospital days.) Suppose that the demand function for visits to doctors has three arguments: health, income, and the net price paid by the patient (the difference between the fee charged by the physician and the third-party insurance payment made by the person's health insurance carrier). Improvements in health lower the demand, increases in income raise it, and increases in the net price reduce it. The supply function for this market is difficult to specify, but it is sufficient for present purposes to assume that the per capita supply of physicians' services did not decrease between 1972 and 1980. Over these years family income rose;[14] health insurance coverage increased;[15] and per capita visits to doctors declined. We find it hard to reconcile these facts with the hypothesis that average male health declined between 1972 and 1980. Our conclusion is that the declines in per capita visits to doctors and in hospital days probably reflect more than improved health. They may also reflect such factors as market pressure and government controls.

A decline in death rates, such as has recently occurred in the United States, results in a larger population. The marginal survivors may have poorer average health than others of the same age. If declining death rates are on a large scale and cover a long period, the number of marginal survivors with below-average health can become

TABLE 6–5
Objective Measures of Health of the Male Population, by Age Group, 1972 and 1980

	Mortality Rate (per 1,000 persons)			Average Number of Visits to Doctors in Past Twelve Months			Average Number of Hospital Days in Past Twelve Months		
	1972	1980	Change	1972	1980	Change	1972	1980	Change
16–19	1.6	1.4	-0.2	2.22	2.17	-0.05	0.39	0.41	0.02
20–24	2.2	2.0	-0.2	2.47	2.16	-0.31	0.61	0.53	-0.08
25–34	2.1	2.0	-0.1	2.51	2.43	-0.08	0.66	0.55	-0.11
35–44	3.9	3.0	-0.9	2.82	2.68	-0.14	0.87	0.86	-0.01
45–54	9.4	7.7	-1.7	3.42	3.03	-0.39	1.42	1.19	-0.23
55–59	18.1	14.6	-3.5	3.81	3.93	0.12	1.92	1.77	-0.15
60–64	27.5	22.3	-5.2	4.49	4.20	-0.29	2.07	1.87	-0.20
65–69	40.0	33.9	-6.1	4.86	4.11	-0.75	2.50	2.27	-0.23
70+	92.5	82.2	-10.3	5.47	4.78	-0.69	3.65	2.91	-0.74
16+	14.3	12.3	-2.0	3.24	2.98	-0.26	1.29	1.11	-0.18
16+, fixed age weights[a]	14.4	12.3	-2.1	3.22	2.98	-0.24	1.27	1.11	-0.16

a. 1980 age weights use to reweight 1972 data.
SOURCES: Mortality rates from U.S. Department of Health and Human Services, *Vital Statistics 1980*, vol. 2, *Mortality*. Visits to doctors and hospital days based on tabulations of the Health Interview Survey conducted at the Urban Institute. Hospital days include all hospital visits except mental, tuberculosis, orthopedic, contagious disease, chronic disease, "all other," nursing home, and visits not in the HIS index.

sufficiently large to affect average health. Two recent papers have examined this question.[16] Although their results are not definitive, one of their findings is important. The absolute (not the relative) decline in the death rate must be large for the marginal survivors to become an important fraction of a population cohort. Thus the age group seventy and older is the best candidate for discerning the effects of lower death rates on average health. These effects are unlikely to be important among men in the early retirement years of fifty-five to fifty-nine and sixty to sixty-four.

To summarize, the data on self-reported health and the objective data suggest that the average health of U.S. men did not decline between 1972 and 1980. A situation of roughly constant average health among men of early retirement years is suggested by the health indicators.

The HIS also asks questions about the usual activity of each household member. Possible responses include working, going to school, taking care of the home, retired for health reasons, retired for all other reasons, and a residual "all other" category. Table 6–6 focuses on the responses concerning work and retirement for the years 1972 and 1980. The retirement questions are asked only of persons forty-five and older.

Several points stand out. The proportion of men who report working as their usual activity declined for all adult age groups from those twenty-five to thirty-four to those seventy and older. The largest decline occurred among men sixty to sixty-four (13.7 percentage points). Note also, however, that among men fifty-five to fifty-nine the proportion declined by 5.1 percentage points. In the five oldest groups, the decline in the proportion working was roughly matched by an increase in the proportion retired for all reasons. This decline in labor supply mirrors the declines previously noted. Retirement for health reasons accounted for 69 percent of the increased retirement among men fifty-five to fifty-nine and for 46 percent of the increase among men sixty to sixty-four during the 1972–1980 period.

The data seem to indicate that a substantial proportion of early retirement among men aged fifty-five to sixty-four is for health reasons. This pattern is strikingly similar to the pattern that appears in the work experience data of table 6–3 for the years 1969 to 1979. Unlike those data, however, these are based on a survey that provides objective and subjective measures of the same person's health, and they do not suggest that the average health of older men has deteriorated—even though the men report more early retirement for health reasons.

The HIS data present a paradox with respect to the reasons for

TABLE 6-6
Usual Activity of the Male Population, by Age Group, 1972 and 1980
(percent)

	Working			Retired, All Reasons			Retired, Health Reasons		
	1972	1980	Change	1972	1980	Change	1972	1980	Change
16–19	18.7	23.0	4.3	NA	NA	NA	NA	NA	NA
20–24	70.4	75.4	5.0	NA	NA	NA	NA	NA	NA
25–34	92.6	91.8	−0.8	NA	NA	NA	NA	NA	NA
35–44	95.0	93.3	−1.7	NA	NA	NA	NA	NA	NA
45–54	92.1	90.1	−2.0	3.2	4.7	1.5	2.6	3.6	1.0
55–59	86.1	81.0	−5.1	8.0	13.5	5.5	6.1	9.9	3.8
60–64	73.9	60.2	−13.7	21.5	35.4	13.9	10.9	17.3	6.4
65–69	35.4	27.1	−8.3	61.2	70.4	9.2	18.1	21.1	3.0
70+	14.5	12.7	−1.8	81.4	83.6	2.2	17.8	15.3	−2.5
16+	71.7	70.7	−1.0	11.4	13.6	2.2	3.7	4.4	0.7
16+, fixed age weights[a]	72.0	70.7	−1.3	11.6	13.6	2.0	3.7	4.4	0.7

NA = not applicable. This question was not asked of persons younger than forty-five.
a. 1980 age weights used to reweight the 1972 data.
Source: Based on tabulations of the Health Interview Survey conducted at the Urban Institute.

early retirement. If men are enjoying no worse health, why are they increasingly citing health as their reason for retirement? One explanation may be that before the 1980s these men rationalized not working by citing health reasons, which were socially acceptable. This phenomenon appears to be waning; the data suggest a convergence of reported reasons and actual reasons since 1980. This finding supports the view that early retirement is becoming more socially acceptable. To pursue this question further, the HIS has other health indicators, such as limitations on physical activity and detailed questions on chronic illness or disability. Our attention, however, now shifts to what we believe is a more fruitful line of investigation: income transfers and early retirement.

Income Support Payments and Early Retirement

Since 1969 older men have increasingly become recipients of income support payments from public disability and retirement programs and from private pensions. Data from the Current Population Survey are most useful for documenting this change. The CPS has asked questions about the receipt of welfare, unemployment, disability, and retirement income payments for seven broad categories of programs in every year since 1969.[17] The data include information about the receipt of transfer payments by each member of the household during the previous calendar year.

Substantial numbers of older men receive one or more transfer payments. Summary data for 1969 and 1983 are presented in table 6–7. For both men fifty-five to fifty-nine and those sixty to sixty-four the proportions who received one or more kinds of transfer nearly doubled between 1969 and 1983, increasing from 16.2 to 31.8 percent and from 28.8 to 55.8 percent. Discussions of retirement policy frequently assume that workers retire at sixty-five, but the data vividly illustrate the increasing receipt of transfer income before age sixty-five. Over half the men sixty to sixty-four now receive one or more kinds of income support payments.

The social security disability insurance (DI) program grew rapidly in the late 1960s and early 1970s. Despite major cutbacks in the number of DI beneficiaries in 1981 and 1982, recipiency rates among older men are far higher in the 1980s than they were in the late 1960s.[18] The proportion of men fifty-five to fifty-nine with DI benefits reported in the CPS rose from 4.0 percent in 1969 to 7.3 percent in 1983. Among men sixty to sixty-four the increased percentage of social security beneficiaries reflects both DI and early retirement beneficiaries.

TABLE 6–7

OLDER MEN RECEIVING TRANSFER PAYMENTS, BY AGE GROUP,

1969 AND 1983

(percent)

	45–54	55–59	60–64	65 and Older
All transfers				
1969	15.3	16.2	28.8	81.5
1983	21.0	31.8	55.8	95.5
Change, 1969–1983				
(percentage points)	5.7	15.6	27.0	14.0
Social security and railroad retirement				
1969	1.9	4.0	17.1	74.5
1983	3.2	7.3	31.7	91.3
Change, 1969–1983				
(percentage points)	1.3	3.3	14.6	16.8
Government pensions[a]				
1969	1.4	1.8	3.2	6.4
1983	4.4	7.8	12.5	12.7
Change, 1969–1983				
(percentage points)	3.0	6.0	9.3	6.3
Private pensions				
1969	0.6	2.0	5.9	17.7
1983	1.4	7.0	16.9	30.8
Change, 1969–1983				
(percentage points)	0.8	5.0	11.0	13.1

a. Includes federal civilian pensions, military retirement, and state and local government pensions.
SOURCE: Based on tabulations of the CPS done at the Urban Institute.

Two other kinds of retirement benefits have become increasingly common among these two age groups. Civilian government pensions (federal, state, and local) are often available at fifty-five for persons who also satisfy the years-of-service requirements. Military retirees can receive pension benefits at even earlier ages. Growth in receipt of both government and private pensions was very rapid between 1969 and 1983. This undoubtedly reflects both the lowering of the early retirement age to fifty-five and special "bridge" arrangements or early retirement windows that allow older workers to collect pension benefits (sometimes with less than the full actuarial reduction) before the normal age of eligibility for early retirement specified in private pension plans. In 1983, 7 percent of men fifty-five to fifty-nine and almost 17 percent of men sixty to sixty-four received private pension benefits.[19]

The three programs identified in the table were providing income payments to substantial numbers of older men by 1983. The increases in recipiency rates at ages fifty-five to sixty-four undoubtedly account for much of the decline in labor force attachment documented in this paper. Each of the programs has eligibility conditions that can be satisfied by substantial numbers of men before they reach sixty-two, much less sixty-five. Many private pensions and public employee retirement programs now specify fifty-five (along with a years-of-service requirement) as the minimum retirement age. Men who satisfy these requirements are exercising established property rights. When we examine the programs individually, we discover plausible reasons why more men are retiring early. Many employers with private pension plans wanted to retain younger workers in the recessionary periods of the mid-1970s and the early 1980s and thus made special pension arrangements available to their older workers. Federal civil servants can retire at fifty-five if they satisfy years-of-service requirements.

What is surprising is that so many men are retiring early. They are not waiting until sixty-five but are leaving in their late fifties and early sixties. From the data examined we conclude that average health has not worsened. Rather, it appears that eligibility for income support payments is the principal reason for the increase in early retirement. This is consistent with the economic theory presented and is probably reinforced by changing social attitudes toward retirement.

Conclusions

We have sought to explain the exit of older Americans from the work force. Since 1969 one of the dramatic changes in the labor market has been the increase in early retirement. This does not appear to be due to worsening health of persons fifty-five and older despite increases in the number of retired persons who cite health as the reason for their retirement. Rather, it appears to be primarily a response to the increased availability of retirement and disability benefits.

We offer two final observations. First, changes that raised the mandatory retirement age (for example, from sixty-five to seventy in 1978) and future changes designed to facilitate part-time employment may have very small effects on retirement, the former because so much retirement is taking place before age sixty-five and the latter because so much is taking the form of complete withdrawal from the labor force. Second, if we wanted to reverse the trend toward early retirement, changes in the eligibility conditions for retirement and disability transfers and changes in the size of those transfers might have larger effects. Such changes might include full taxation of OASDHI benefits, more pension offsets (such as offsets involving military pensions), and increases in the minimum age of eligibility for early retirement benefits. Full taxation of OASDHI benefits would reduce expected retirement income for many older persons and might cause some to postpone retirement. Pension offsets that partially reduce payments from one pension when another is received at the same time also reduce retirement income.

Of course, changing financial incentives to work longer may have only a moderate effect on retirement. Nevertheless, we think that public policies can be devised that would make early retirement less attractive financially. Obviously such suggestions are easier to make than to enact because they would change established property rights. Finally, we should reemphasize that even if such policy changes were made, they might have quite small effects in a society where early retirement is an objective of many citizens.

Notes

1. For a description of the 1983 Social Security Amendments, see John Svahn and Mary Ross, "Social Security Amendments of 1983: Legislative History and Summary of Provisions," *Social Security Bulletin* (July 1983), pp. 3–48.

2. U.S. Bureau of the Census, *Historical Statistics of the United States* (Washington, D.C., 1975), p. 132.

3. Annual labor force participation rates from 1947 to 1979 are published in U.S. Department of Labor, *Employment and Training Report of the President, 1980* (Washington, D.C., 1980). Data for 1984 were available in *Employment and Earnings* (January 1985).

4. For a summary of work experience in 1969, see U.S. Department of Labor, Bureau of Labor Statistics, *Work Experience of the Population in 1969*, Special Labor Force Report 127 (Washington, D.C., 1971).

5. For a recent analysis of the retirement test in social security, see Wayne Vroman, "Some Economic Effects of the Social Security Retirement Test," *Research in Labor Economics* (1985). Part 2 of that paper describes the evolution of earnings test provisions from 1950 to 1983.

6. Ibid.; and Wayne Vroman, *Older Worker Earnings and the 1965 Social Security Amendments*, Research Report no. 38 (Washington, D.C.: Social Security Administration, 1971).

7. Vroman, "Some Economic Effects."

8. For a more detailed discussion of lifetime labor supply, see Gary Burtless and Robert A. Moffitt, "The Effect of Social Security Benefits on the

Labor Supply of the Aged," in Henry Aaron and Gary Burtless, eds., *Retirement and Economic Behavior* (Washington, D.C.: Brookings Institution, 1984); and Frank J. Sammartino, "The Effect of Health on Retirement" (Working paper prepared for the Retirement Age Study, April 1985).

9. An example of a simple model of lifetime labor supply is the following. Let $U(T-R,Y)$ be a person's utility function, where T is the life expectancy, R is the number of years of work (or retirement date), $T-R$ is the number of years of retirement, and Y is the present value of lifetime income. This present value can be expressed as

$$Y = (W/r)\,(1 - e^{-rR}) + (1/r)[A + b(W,R)](e^{-rR} - e^{-rT})$$

where r is the discount rate; W is annual preretirement earnings, assumed for simplicity to be constant; A is annual retirement income that does not depend on the person's prior work history; and $b(W,R)$ is the portion of retirement income that depends on preretirement earnings or the number of years of work or both. Both W and R are assumed to raise retirement income, that is, $b_1>0$ and $b_2>0$. For the sake of simplicity, assume that the function $b(W,R)$ is linear: $b(W,R) = b_1 W + b_2 R$. The first-order condition for the maximization of the utility function subject to the equation above for Y can then be used to derive the effects of the parameters W, A, b_1, b_2, and T on the age of retirement.

10. This result is reversed when the person is in a situation in which a one-dollar increase in annual salary results in a more than one-dollar increase in retirement benefits. This is likely only for very low-wage workers who receive the minimum social security benefit or those whose payments include dependents' allowances.

11. One recent summary and evaluation of this literature is Sammartino, "The Effect of Health."

12. For one description of the HIS, see U.S. Department of Health and Human Services, National Center for Health Statistics, *Current Estimates from the National Health Interview Survey: United States, 1980*, Series 10, no. 139 (Washington, D.C., 1981). The HIS interviews a nationally representative sample of about 40,000 households each year. Extract files from the HIS for the years 1972 and 1980 have been tabulated at the Urban Institute. These two years were chosen because they were the earliest and latest years for which there were questions about self-assessments of health in the HIS.

13. See U.S. Department of Health and Human Services, *Vital Statistics 1980*, vol. 2, *Mortality* (Washington, D.C., 1985), pt. A, table 1.3.

14. See Executive Office of the President, *Economic Report of the President, 1985* (Washington, D.C., 1985), table B34. Per capita real disposable income rose from $3,860 in 1972 to $4,487 in 1980, an increase of 16.2 percent.

15. See Katherine Swartz, "Who Has Been without Health Insurance? Changes between 1963 and 1979" (Working paper no. 3308-01, Urban Institute, April 1984), table 1. Swartz shows estimates of health insurance coverage among persons younger than sixty-five. The coverage percentages were 69.6 in 1963, 86.1 in 1976, and 85.7 in 1979. Since 1979 the percentage of the population with health insurance coverage has declined slightly.

16. Martin N. Baily, "Aging and Ability to Work: Policy Issues and Recent Trends" (Paper presented at Brookings Conference on Retirement and Aging, Washington, D.C., May 1985); and James M. Poterba and Lawrence H. Summers, "Public Policy Implications of Declining Old-Age Mortality" (Paper presented at Brookings Conference on Retirement and Aging, Washington, D.C., May 1985).

17. The seven categories are public assistance (Aid to Families with Dependent Children, Supplemental Security Income, and general assistance), unemployment insurance, workers compensation, veterans' benefits, social security (OASDHI plus railroad retirement), government pensions (federal civilian, military retirement, and state and local government), and private pensions.

18. The number of DI beneficiaries (including dependents) declined from 4.78 million at the end of 1980 to 3.81 million at the end of 1983—a reduction of 20.3 percent.

19. The pension benefits reported in the CPS are payments made in periodic installments. Because one-time severance pension payments are not recorded in the CPS, it substantially understates the total dollar amount and the number of pension recipients. In 1980, for example, pension income as reported in the CPS was only 64 percent of the amount shown in the National Income Accounts (table 6.14).

7
Reforming Medicare and Medicaid

Jack A. Meyer

A new approach to Medicare and Medicaid that would fill unmet social needs for the elderly and create a complementary relationship between government health care programs and private sector initiatives is clearly necessary.

Medicare and Medicaid are essentially good programs. What they have set out to do, they have generally done well. Both programs have increased access to health care, fulfilling their most important social goal. But they are somewhat lopsided and unbalanced. Medicaid covers some people very well but bypasses others with equal or greater needs. Medicare covers everyone in the potentially eligible population group sixty-five and over, but covers some health services completely while leaving the elderly almost totally vulnerable for the cost of other health services. Medicaid pays for nearly everything for only half of the population in need, while Medicare pays for about half the cost of health care for the whole population in need.

Lurking beneath these gaps and imbalances is the troubling, costly problem of financing long-term care for the elderly. Other chapters in this volume outline the important potential role of private sector initiatives, such as group insurance and continuing care retirement communities, in meeting long-term-care needs. This chapter outlines some fundamental revisions in Medicare and Medicaid that would build a more complete catastrophic protection feature into government programs—one that does not shy away from long-term care.

Various ways of leveraging limited new government outlays—or retargeting existing funds—to improve coverage and foster better private protection are discussed. There has been too much partisan bickering and ideological debate over whether our growing long-term-care needs should be met through either a major new government program or purely private approaches. I believe we need a combination of a more active private role and redesigned public sector programs. And the crucial factor will be how these efforts mesh.

For example, if a true stop-loss feature can be built into the public sector health care programs, it would probably stimulate the types of

103

private initiatives discussed elsewhere in this volume. Thus, this chapter is meant not to stand apart from the other contributions to the book, but to serve as a bridge that connects those chapters to a discussion of Medicare and Medicaid. It explains how we could achieve a better fit between public and private sector coverage for the elderly's health services.

The chapter has three major goals: (1) to analyze the basic flaws in our current public programs for health care; (2) to develop a new policy strategy for correcting the flaws and improving the programs; and (3) to outline alternative ways to finance the new agenda.

The Flaws in Our Current System

This section outlines some of the limitations and problems in the current Medicare and Medicaid programs, focusing on the elderly and emphasizing the lack of adequate protection for catastrophic expenses in general and for long-term care in particular.

Insurance Coverage for Long-Term Care Is Limited. Health insurance often stops at the hospital door; Medicare provides limited coverage for postacute care in an institutional setting (for example, 150 days in a skilled-nursing facility with a high copayment after the twentieth day). Medicaid kicks in only after patients have spent nearly all their assets, and then coverage is mainly for care in a nursing home.

Thus, insurance coverage is tied to institutional care and forces many people into a difficult choice between moving into an institution and getting little or no care. Government help not only is tied to institutional care, but also provides everything to the pauperized patient and nothing to the patient with assets beyond a token amount. Thus, the two primary features of government aid for long-term care are the requirement of institutionalization and the "welfarizing" of the assistance. Both features need to be changed.

Coverage for home care under Medicare and Medicaid is quite limited and is tied to services ordered by physicians for those on a clear path to recovery. It is more oriented to equipment than to custodial needs.

In 1982 only 5.5 percent of the disabled elderly received formal care alone (for example, care in a nursing home or care provided by a doctor or a home health agency). About three-fourths of them (73.9 percent) received only informal care (for example, the assistance provided by a family member), while the remaining one-fifth (20.6 percent) received a mixture of formal and informal care.[1] Thus, in the important area of disability, Medicare and Medicaid, which cover

104

mainly formal care, are zeroing in on the smallest part of the population in need.

The bitter irony here is that despite the roughly $130 billion per year in federal and state outlays, Medicare and Medicaid are often not there when the elderly really need them. The programs also have a bias against care delivered outside the institutional setting. They originally embodied a poorly conceived cost-based reimbursement system as well. Here, at least, the federal government can point with pride to some real progress in recent years in the restructuring of hospital payment. Physician payment under Medicare remains inefficient and cost-generating, however, and is badly in need of reform.

The programs established by the federal government in 1966 reflected the system that was prevalent in the private sector. In fact, transporting that system, with its biases toward front-end coverage, institutional care, and cost-based reimbursement, from the world of private insurance into the new public programs was a part of the deal that enabled Medicare to be enacted.

Private insurance for long-term care is also quite limited. Generally speaking, it rounds out and fills in what Medicare covers but does not complement Medicare and Medicaid adequately. Private coverage mirrors public programs in many ways, adopting some of the same coverage restrictions found in the public sector. Private coverage for home care is also limited, particularly for custodial care. Private coverage for institutional care is time-limited (for example, three years in a nursing home) and often requires a prior hospitalization.

Both Medicare and private insurance are biased in favor of covering acute care. Although there are copayments and deductibles for acute care, coverage is extensive. Under Medicare, the elderly are responsible for so-called front-end (or initial) costs, but about two-thirds have private medigap insurance to cover those costs. Another significant percentage have the Medicaid coverage that helps them with the deductible and copayments under Medicare. Many poor elderly are, however, screened out of qualifying for this Medicaid match, and the near-poor elderly often fall between the public safety net and supplemental coverage.

Nonetheless, coverage for acute care has been relatively solid, and it has recently become more extensive. Congress passed major legislation in May 1988 that provides catastrophic coverage for the acute care part of Medicare. The new law places limits on out-of-pocket outlays for hospital charges and doctor bills of about $2,000 per year. It also provides partial Medicare reimbursement for prescription drug costs that exceed $600 per year. The law contains only limited new coverage for long-term care. For example, it increases skilled nursing facility coverage under Medicare from 100 to 150 days while lowering the copayment responsibility of the patient. It also permits the spouse of a publicly supported nursing home patient to retain an income level that avoids impoverishment. The new provisions on long-term care, however, extend Medicare's coverage of long-term care at the front end of need while leaving catastrophic expenses uncovered.

The catastrophic coverage law also improves Medicaid coverage for the elderly poor by extending it to the poor even if they are ineligible for the Supplemental Security Income (SSI) cash assistance program. This is a worthy step and one that I favor. The point is that catastrophic protection is largely for acute care needs.

Both public and private health care coverage are still tied to the standard medical model and to care given in an institutional setting. Yet we know that the need is increasingly occurring outside institutional settings and outside the traditional medical model. Of course, we need standard medicine and basic research. But we also need greater emphasis on gerontology, social services, and support for families providing long-term care to a relative.

The Payment System in Health Care Is Fragmented. Besides being biased toward acute care and institutional settings, Medicare's coverage and payment system is fragmented. This fragmentation is a particular problem for the elderly because their high incidence of chronic health care needs requires an integrated system that includes both acute and long-term-care services.

Insurers operate in the world of diagnosis-related groups (DRGs)—or rapidly emerging private sector counterparts—for hospital costs, and still other systems for paying doctors (even for work done in the hospital), for immediate post-acute or transitional care, and for nursing homes and longer-term home care. In recent years, the federal government has begun to contract with health maintenance organizations (HMOs) and other competitive medical plans that offer more integrated benefits. But there are clear limits to how many elderly people could or would enroll in the country's limited number of HMOs (currently about 600). Instead of pushing HMOs to the exclusion of other cost-effective health plans that are "hybrids" of the prepaid care and fee-for-service models, the federal government should open its Medicare contracting to a broader spectrum of plans. In a pluralistic environment, the elderly would have a choice of HMOs, independent practice associations, preferred provider plans, and even standard fee-for-service plans that incorporate more utilization review and other efforts to hold down acute care costs.

Although HMOs are not the only way to obtain better integration of benefits, preliminary evaluations of HMOs providing benefits to the Medicare population offer promising signs. Researchers evaluated twenty-six prepaid plans under contract with Medicare between 1982 and 1985. They found that hospital use is lower for the beneficiaries in these plans than for others in the fee-for-service system and that most of the HMOs generated surpluses and used them to provide additional benefits.[2] Some HMOs, for example, are offering unlimited hospital and nursing home days in addition to extra coverage for prescription drugs and refraction/audiometric services. Others are offering plans with no premium requirements or premiums below Medicare's Part B requirement.

Innovative experiments are operating around the borders of the Medicare program. But in the more traditional and still prevalent model, providers survive financially by moving patients on to the next part of a fragmented system. The name of the game is to get them through the hospital gate and into another institution or setting. For example, nothing in the financial structure of the Medicare payment system makes it financially attractive for a provider to keep a patient hospitalized a little longer (perhaps in a "step-down" or lighter-care setting) even when that might avert substantial costs after the patient leaves, or prevent readmission.

The Federal Tax System Does Not Adequately Encourage Families to Provide Either Transitional or Long-Term Care. There is no tax credit for elder care that is analogous to the child-care credit. Yet, like child care, elder care can inhibit work performance. In addition, current law provides a deduction to a household that is responsible for half or more of the expenses of a person who is judged dependent. This creates a "notch" problem, with no incentive to help fund care that will amount to less than half of total expenses.

Medicare Coverage Is Confusing. Many people still believe they are covered for more long-term care than they are. Clearly there is need for accurate information about Medicare and private insurance coverage. Employers can contribute by educating workers about future coverage, and Medicare can do a better job of informing beneficiaries. In addition, it is difficult to find a single source of information about available health and related social services. There is a need for information clearinghouses as well as for more coordination of the services themselves.

Long-term care encompasses an array of medical and nonmedical social services. Many of the needs are for personal care, custodial care, and companionship—needs that are not readily filled or covered by most government programs. Where they are covered, it is in a patchwork pattern. One program under the Social Services Block Grant covers a particular need, another program under the Older Americans Act covers something else, while Medicaid covers yet a third need—often differently, depending on the state.

In addition, numerous state and local government programs are available, and dozens of private sector organizations deliver social services to disabled or homebound elderly people. A recent study of home care in New York City, for example, found that more than 200 organizations offered some form of home-care services in 1986. Among these were at least 100 businesses, 61 nonprofit personal care agencies, and 36 nonprofit certified home health agencies.[3] Selecting from the complex array of potential services a package that can be tailored to the needs of a single patient can be a daunting task, either for the patient or for the patient's family members.

Facilities and Services for Long-Term Care Are in Short Supply in Some Areas. Health planning agencies and states have put lids on the delivery system, in an effort to control costs by controlling supply. Freezing market entry not only leads to shortages and waiting lists, but also thwarts innovation. Certificate-of-need (CON) programs became a capital protection device that insulated those already in the system from those seeking entry. This process underwrites inefficiency in health service delivery. The health care industry is overbuilt because we have long relied on faulty payment systems and ineffective planning mechanisms designed to slow down industry growth. But the answer to this problem is not to close the front door, blocking the replacement of less efficient facilities by more efficient ones.

Besides undesirable entry controls, obsolete or self-serving licensure requirements limit competition among groups of professionals, thus restricting the supply of services. The overprofessionalization of services that results from unduly restrictive licensure requirements is a particular problem for long-term care, so much of which does not require highly skilled personnel.

Ensuring quality does not necessarily require that everyone who helps the elderly have a master's degree. For many tasks, continuity of care, vigilance, and caring itself may be more important than the precise training of the care giver. Other tasks may require formal or technical training, but tasks such as helping with bathing or turning a patient in bed are increasingly important. And many patients need to be taken to the doctor, while others need companionship or someone to check with them regularly. Our system is not well equipped to meet these needs. But the solution is not simply to expand government programs into these areas. Government should not move in with front-end funding for every social and medical service.

There Is Too Much Economic Regulation, Too Little Quality Assurance Monitoring. Along with relaxing strictures against market entry, we need to develop clear standards for the quality of transitional and long-term care provided in hospitals (for example, swing beds), nursing homes, board and care facilities, and other settings. In other words, instead of freezing the market, we should thaw it out, guarding against abuse through a combination of public and private performance standards instead of rigid, inflexible design standards. An open market with reasonable performance standards is far preferable to a closed or overly restrictive market. A strategy for cost containment based on rate and entry controls will work no better in health care than it has worked in other sectors of our economy such as airlines, trucking, and financial services.

Many Elderly Lack Resources to Pay for Uninsured Health Care Out of-Pocket. Long-term care is extremely expensive. Nursing home costs typically range from $20,000 to $40,000 per year. Even a few weeks of visiting nurses, therapists, or paid companionship can amount to a sizable amount of money. Medicare coverage can be quickly exhausted, and Medicaid does not help until resources are almost totally dried up. And many home-care services, as noted earlier, are not covered by private insurance.

Out-of-pocket costs for acute care can also mount up and pose a great burden on lower-income Medicare beneficiaries. Indeed, 28.5 percent of the elderly with incomes below $5,000 in 1985 lacked both Medicaid and private supplementary coverage.[4] A recent General Accounting Office (GAO) study examined out-of-pocket cost increases for all types of health services, including acute and long-term care. The GAO report found that after adjusting for inflation, budget and tax bills passed between 1980 and 1985 led to a 49 percent increase in out-of-pocket payments by Medicare beneficiaries for hospital, home, and skilled-nursing-facility care. The GAO study also found that out-of-pocket costs after Medicare's payment of physician charges, lab fees, and outpatient hospital services rose, in real terms, by 31 percent over this period.

109

Policy Strategy to Improve Publicly Financed Care for the Elderly

This section develops a policy strategy to improve the Medicare program and the portion of Medicaid covering the elderly. The emphasis is on revisions that build a true catastrophic expense protection feature into public programs for long-term care and on achieving a better fit between public programs and private sector financing arrangements.

Greater coordination and integration of acute and long-term-care health coverage would require an incentive structure that rewards the insurer or provider for good results, such as recovery from illness or prevention of disease. Achieving savings in the acute health system and applying them to long-term-care coverage is crucial to this strategy. This is happening now under Medicare risk-sharing contracts with HMOs and competitive medical plans, and is being tested in the social HMO experiments.

We should also experiment with the coordinated management of health benefits in these key areas:

- Medicare and employer-provided retiree health benefits
- Medicare and Medicaid coverage for dual eligibles
- Medicare and private medigap policies

Payment and delivery system reforms are a prerequisite to additional financing. It would be a mistake to pour new money into a fragmented system that is biased toward high-cost institutional care without first—or at least simultaneously—reforming the finance and delivery systems to correct some of their flaws.

Reforming Medicare and Medicaid. Reforms in the coverage of long-term care under public programs could be built along two separate lines. First, the Medicaid program could be modified to provide better coverage for long-term care in a vertical direction—that is, reaching up the income and asset ladder. The descent into abject poverty that now must precede any coverage under Medicaid for long-term care would be better cushioned, with graduated subsidies and more asset protection. A second approach, discussed in the next section, could redesign Medicare to integrate it better with private insurance.

There are several problems with the Medicaid expansion approach. First, we must be cautious about providing too much asset protection. We do not want middle- and low-to-moderate-income taxpayers paying more taxes to protect the assets of those with greater resources. But between that inequitable situation and today's debilitating "free fall," there is plenty of room for reform.

Another problem with Medicaid expansion is that it would cost both federal and state governments a great deal of money. Raising the asset limit for eligibility from $2,000 to the range of $10,000 to $15,000, coupled with expanding Medicaid policies horizontally (that is, allowing Medicaid to cover a greater proportion of the poor elderly) is likely to cost about $15 to $20 billion per year. For a vastly overextended federal government, a one-step major new financing commitment for Medicaid expansion is probably unrealistic. Another drawback of this approach is that it continues the emphasis on means testing and public welfare, which ultimately could be deleterious to building support for a long-range solution for this problem.

An alternative approach to pure Medicaid expansion involves state efforts to waive the Medicaid spend-down requirement for an individual who purchases a private insurance policy covering a minimum set of long-term-care benefits. After a purchaser of such a private policy paid its deductibles and exhausted its benefits, the purchaser would automatically be eligible for Medicaid.

Instead of a major expansion of Medicaid to cover the near-poor and those with low or moderate resources (vertical expansion), we should take incremental steps to make the program more equitable horizontally. It would thus do a better job of fully covering the elderly poverty population. The catastrophic illness protection legislation provides a start in this direction by:

• Mandating Medicaid buy-in protection for Medicare beneficiaries with incomes below the federal poverty line, regardless of SSI participation. Medicaid will now pay the Medicare premiums, deductibles, and copayments for more of the elderly poor.

• Increasing the personal needs allowance from its current low level of $25 per month.

• Liberalizing the income and asset restrictions on a community-based spouse of a nursing home patient. This step will provide some "vertical" protection above the poverty line, but only for couples.

These steps have improved Medicaid coverage directly by changing some of the program parameters. An effort could also be made to improve coverage for long-term care by bringing more people into the SSI program and raising SSI benefits. The following steps should be taken:

• Drop the 209b provision of federal law that permits states to set more restrictive criteria for Medicaid eligibility than for SSI eligibility. Everyone who is eligible for SSI should be eligible for Medicaid. About 22 percent of the SSI population live in fourteen states that exercise this 209b option.

111

- Develop a more effective outreach program to increase participation in SSI among those who are eligible. Only about half of those eligible now participate.
- Raise SSI benefits, in stages if necessary, to federal poverty thresholds.
- Relax the SSI asset test; note that this is an alternative to easing the Medicaid asset test. If we doubled the SSI asset limits, the yearly cost would probably be in the $50 to $60 million range.

The precise cost for these steps depends on a variety of factors, such as which poverty line is used (elderly or overall) and how much the asset test is relaxed. I estimate that such a package would cost about $6 billion per year *when fully implemented*. Of course it would be possible to implement the plan in stages or to fill in the gaps partially instead of fully. A package of helpful changes could be put together at several alternative funding levels.

The final section of this chapter lays out the broad contours of some basic options for financing these steps; my 1987 study with Sheila Zedlewski analyzes these financing options in more detail.[5]

A New Approach to Long-Term Care under Medicare

An alternative to Medicaid expansion is to reform Medicare to provide greater protection for long-term-care. I do not favor simply adding to Medicare a major long-term-care program that starts at the front end of need and has little or no coinsurance. This approach would remove the incentive of families to provide for themselves. The cost of such a "blank check" program would break the federal bank.

Furthermore, available forecasts indicate that the federal government will be lucky to meet its current Medicare commitments in the early part of the next century when demographic forces really take hold. The steps I recommend could require some new spending. They could also be accomplished through a redirection of outlays, better targeting, and a new approach to Medicare that makes it a more complete catastrophic protection program.

The new approach presented here uses either the Medicare program or the federal tax system to create a stop-loss provision that protects families from extremely high long-term-care costs. Instead of offering only generous hospital coverage, reasonably good physician coverage, and little long-term-care protection, as Medicare does today, the federal government should provide full across-the-board protection against financial ruin. With the federal government as a backstop, there would be much more interest in private sector insurance for long-term care.

The reforms outlined here deal directly with the lopsided nature of the current Medicare program. For example, open-heart surgery that costs $25,000 may be fully covered, while long-term-care expenses of $25,000 are almost totally unreimbursed. Both Medicare and the private insurance industry seem to vie for the part of catastrophic coverage related to acute care, but to steer clear of the part relating to long-term care.

If the federal government provided a measure of back-end, across-the-board coverage for long-term-care services, insurers and prepaid plans would be more willing to provide coverage at the front end and in the middle through redesigned insurance and delivery packages. HMOs, for example, might be much more amenable to taking higher-risk older persons and extending some coverage for long-term care if they knew that Medicare would serve as a backstop on catastrophic long-term-care expenses.

There are three ways to establish this new federal role. First, Medicare could set up a new entitlement for long-term care, but with a substantial waiting period—say two or three years—and substantial coinsurance, which Medicaid would pay for those who are poor. Second, Medicare could reinsure the private market against very high expenses, perhaps over $100,000. Third, the U.S. government could provide refundable tax credits for long-term-care expenses that exceed some proportion of income.

Certain conditions would need to be present, however, for Medicare to serve either as an entitlement in this area or as a reinsurer: (1) a clear definition of the degree of disability that qualifies a person for benefits, one that limits coverage to rather serious levels of impairment; (2) significant deductibles and copayments; and (3) a waiting period. Analogous conditions would need to be developed if the government adopted a tax credit approach.

The advantage to these approaches is that a household would not necessarily have to spend down into poverty to obtain coverage for long-term care. Everyone with substantial disabilities would qualify for this benefit after expending a significant amount of resources. This would make government assistance for long-term care a universal benefit and steer clear of a welfare image.

It has been estimated that a public long-term catastrophic care insurance program with a three-year deductible would cost the government $6.3 billion annually (in 1987 dollars) in the period from 2016 to 2020. The estimated reduction in Medicaid costs is $23.8 billion, or 51.5 percent (from $46.2 billion to $22.4 billion). The new public insurance would entail $30.1 billion in outlays, or $6.3 billion more than the reduction in Medicaid outlays. The cost of a two-year

113

deductible program has been estimated at $15.7 billion annually (in 1987 dollars) between 2016 and 2020.[6]

These estimates do not make adjustments for increases in utilization that might occur in response to insurance coverage, or what economists call "moral hazard." To the extent that utilization increased, the cost estimates would also rise. Against that, the estimates presumably also do not allow for improvements we might make in case management and community-based care that might help to reduce nursing home utilization. Thus, they more or less take the world as we know it today and project the cost of new insurance coverage into the future. This is a good starting point, but it is only a beginning. One real challenge is to improve both the public and private insurance products now available. Another is to devise better policies in such areas as the integration of benefits between acute and long-term care. Yet a third is to channel patients to care in the most appropriate and cost-effective setting.

If public insurance for long-term care were added to the existing Medicare program, states would gain substantial fiscal relief. The federal government should turn back to the states an equivalent amount of spending obligations under programs in such areas as economic development and transportation. In fact, appropriate expenditure cuts in other areas of the budget would be one way to finance a greater federal role in long-term care.

If Medicare provided a stop-loss feature, federal outlays would also be saved under the Medicaid program (in addition to the savings realized by the states). In my view, such savings should be used for such purposes as strengthening the SSI program along the lines noted earlier. If Medicare "buys out" part of the back end of Medicaid, the resultant Medicaid savings should be used to enhance coverage for the elderly poor at the front end. The recently enacted catastrophic health care legislation sets a precedent for this by using the Medicaid savings from an expansion of Medicare's acute care coverage to extend Medicaid coverage for the elderly poor.

The tax credit plan that I have developed provides back-end coverage once a household has spent more than 10 percent of its adjusted gross income on long-term care. This would be accomplished through a refundable tax credit. All the elderly would be eligible, including those with no federal tax liability.

Under this plan, households could count the full amount of the premium paid for a qualified long-term-care insurance policy toward the 10 percent threshold. They could also count half the expenditures made out-of-pocket for long-term care, up to some annual maximum.

Counting premium payments in full toward the tax credit would encourage people to purchase private long-term-care insurance. Counting half the out-of-pocket outlays up to a cap would preserve the incentive to find economical care—an incentive that disappears under a policy of reimbursing them dollar-for-dollar.

My approach is based on four premises: (1) it is reasonable to expect people to pay a certain portion of their incomes for long-term care; (2) the amount they should have to pay out-of-pocket should be directly related to their ability to pay; (3) government subsidies should encourage private insurance coverage; and (4) government should provide reinsurance or stop-loss protection against the risk of incurring catastrophic expenditures for long-term care.

The advantage of this approach over that taken in the recently enacted catastrophic care bill is that it would target and scale government aid to actual financial need. This need is defined by the relationship between out-of-pocket outlays and income, a true measure of medical indigency. The catastrophic bill puts about a $2,000 annual cap on doctor and hospital bills for all Americans over sixty-five. That cap is too high for some and too low for others and does not even apply to expenditures for long-term care.

A recently defeated congressional proposal for long-term care— H.R. 3436, sponsored by Representative Claude Pepper—repeats that mistake. It would provide up-front coverage for home care while ignoring expenditures for nursing home care, which account for four-fifths of the expenses that exceed $2,000 a year for older Americans.

The approach outlined here would leverage federal dollars to establish a better link between public and private sector insurance coverage. The leveraging technique favored is to provide back-end government stop-loss protection. Government dollars could also be used at the front end by offering premium subsidies in the form of tax credits or deductions for people who purchase a minimum amount of insurance protection. Deductibles and copayments under private insurance could also be subsidized on a sliding scale related to ability to pay.

Relationship of Medicare Changes to Private Sector Reforms. If Medicare is going to provide a greater measure of catastrophic protection, people must prepare themselves to bear more expenses at the front end. The system I favor would have three parts: (1) a Medicare backstop for long-term care; (2) a more secure and equitable public safety net; and (3) personal and family responsibility for what lies in between. In other words, government would send the following message to the public. People should do as much as they can, through insurance and saving during their working years, to prepare themselves for this contingency. If they incur huge expenses related to long-term care for serious disability, Medicare will be there whether they have fully exhausted their resources or not. This help will be in the form of a stop-loss program, public reinsurance that protects their private insurer or prepaid health plan against the possibility of incurring catastrophic outlays or a federal tax credit. If they are poor, a more equitable Medicaid program will help them. But the government cannot run a national asset protection program for all Americans at all asset levels. So if people want to protect their assets above poverty or near-poor levels, they should get insurance.

Among the promising private financing mechanisms are long-term-care insurance and home equity conversion. If employers can offer employees the opportunity to buy long-term-care insurance on a group basis during their working years and help educate them about the need for such coverage, a significant proportion of workers will be able to afford the premium cost. With a more secure Medicare program, there is a greater opportunity to relax the restrictions built into current private insurance, such as marketing to older people on an individual basis instead of to workers in employee groups, requiring prior hospitalization, and excluding people for prior health conditions. In a flexible benefit package, employers could offer aging workers choices and trade-offs in which long-term-care insurance begins to substitute for other benefits, such as life insurance.

The federal government should encourage the spread of private insurance for long-term care through the favorable tax treatment of payments used to prefund long-term-care expenses. Currently, it is unclear whether interest earned on such set-asides would be taxed as it accrues or on a deferred basis. Legislation is needed to clarify the tax treatment of health care, life insurance, and long-term-care prefunding and to make this treatment consistent across various types of benefits.

The total value of home equity for the elderly has been estimated at $700 billion. Elderly homeowners could receive a stream of cash payments that would help defray the costs of long-term care in return for pledging a portion of the equity in their homes. A key to the development of this kind of financial instrument will be the assurance that homeowners will not be forced to abandon their homes if they outlive the term of the mortgage. Experiments that build in this type of safeguard are now in progress.

In addition to these private sector financing mechanisms, we need to tap the voluntary sector's helping network for more assistance in meeting the needs of the frail elderly. Local private sector organizations could play a useful role in coordinating and improving information about available services in their areas. In the present fragmented system, no entity has the incentive to develop such a clearinghouse. We need better discharge planning information and better data on patient health status at periodic intervals after discharge from a hospital or nursing home. There is also a need for a centralized information source about community services that is accessible to the elderly and their families. Moreover, private sector organizations could take a more active role in shaping standards of quality for long-term care.

Private, nonprofit organizations can also play a key role in delivering and monitoring care by organizing volunteer networks for home visits to the elderly and respite care for spouses and children providing long-term care, and by arranging for services such as Meals-on-Wheels or physical therapy. The Retiree Service Volunteer Program (RSVP), the programs of the International Ladies Garment Workers Union, and other similar activities provide the type of caring outreach that can probably never be fully achieved by the medical profession or by a government program.

Finally, the government could make it easier for family members to balance their responsibilities in the workplace with their desire to help care for a spouse or a parent requiring long-term care. One step that could be considered is providing a limited tax credit for workers who use more leave than their jobs entitle them to in order to help provide care to a relative. In other words, if workers' pay were docked because they ran out of leave, they could get a tax break. Current law allows a tax credit for the expenses that a working family incurs to arrange for child care. The elder-care tax credit would be an extension of this concept to care provided by such a family to a senior citizen.

Alternative Methods of Financing New Commitments

Any new commitments on the part of the federal government should be fully funded. It would be fiscally irresponsible to add further to the federal deficit, which is already much too high. In my view, the financing source should also be progressive—we do not want to tax one group of relatively needy people to help another group. Moreover, I believe the financing source should bear some recognizable link to the social objective. This means that in financing new commitments to provide long-term care we should select mechanisms that are associated with the life-cycle process of setting aside money for retirement and health care needs.

The funding mechanism should also promote the concept of generational equity. To the extent that older people are protected against the expenses associated with long-term care, their children and grandchildren will also be helped, and these indirect beneficiaries should be willing to help pay. In addition, these younger people will be older themselves, one day.

The following major options meet the criteria just outlined:

- taxing more of social insurance benefits
- taxing more of employee benefits
- expanding the payroll tax base
- taxing estates more heavily
- cutting government expenditures in ways that protect the needy

Taxing a Greater Portion of Social Security Benefits. The current method of taxing social security benefits counts one-half of the value of benefits as taxable income when certain income thresholds are exceeded: $25,000 for individual and $32,000 for joint returns. One alternative is to tax the amount of social security benefits that exceeds the lifetime contributions by employees plus interest, which is how private pension plan benefits are taxed. This would be approximated by taxing 85 percent of benefits with no income thresholds triggering liability. The cumulative five-year revenue gain between 1989 and 1993 is estimated at $75 billion.[7] If 60 percent of benefits were taxed and the income thresholds were eliminated, the five-year revenue gain would be $44 billion.[8]

Taxing Medicare Benefits. Another option for broadening the tax base by taxing social insurance benefits would be to tax the portion of contributions to Medicare that beneficiaries do *not* make. Beneficiaries now pay one-half of the portion of the payroll tax earmarked for Part A of Medicare and 25 percent of the cost of Part B in the form of a monthly premium. Perhaps 50 percent of the insurance value of Part A benefits, and 75 percent of the insurance value of Part B benefits, could be treated as taxable income for Medicare enrollees. If the current income thresholds for taxing social security benefits were kept in place and applied to these taxable Medicare values, CBO estimates the federal government would receive an additional $17.5 billion between 1989 and 1993.[9]

Taxing Employee Health Benefits. Employer contributions for employee health care benefits are currently tax-free income to the employee. One proposal to limit the exclusion would treat as taxable income any employer contribution to health insurance that exceeds $225 a month for family policies and $90 a month for individual

118

policies (in 1989 dollars, with these amounts indexed for subsequent inflation). Over the five-year period from 1989 through 1993, CBO estimates that the increase in federal revenues would be $47.5 billion. Of this amount, $30.6 billion would be increased income tax revenue, and $16.9 billion would be payroll tax revenue gains.[10]

Increasing the Payroll Tax Base. The limit on income subject to the payroll tax in 1988 is $45,000. Increasing the cap to $75,000 for both employer and employee payments would raise an estimated $13 billion in additional revenues in 1988.[11] Some of the gains would be offset in future years by new commitments to pay additional future benefits to higher-income workers. If the base were raised to $75,000 on employer payments alone (a variation of this option that I do not favor), about $7 billion would be raised in 1988. No added commitments to pay future benefits would be incurred.

Taxing Estates. The estate tax base has eroded in recent years as the threshold value of estates that triggers estate tax liability has risen in stages from $175,625 in 1981 to $600,000 today. As a result, estate tax collections began declining in 1981. The CBO estimates that if the estate tax exemption were lowered to $400,000 and held there, and the current tax rate were frozen, federal revenues would increase by about $9 billion. Under current law, expectations are for revenues from estate and gift taxes to decline steadily from $5.8 billion in 1988 to $3.3 billion in 1992.[12]

We could raise new revenue by taxing capital gains at death. Currently, when a person sells an inherited asset, he or she pays capital gains tax only on the gain since the time of inheritance. The gain accumulated but not realized by the decedent is not taxable to the heir unless it is included in an estate valued at $600,000 or more, where it is subject to the estate tax. Capital gains could be taxed more fully either by taxing them on the decedent's final income tax return or by requiring the beneficiary to carry forward the decedent's cost basis (for example, adjusted original purchase price). CBO estimates that taxing capital gains at death would raise about $21 billion in new revenues over the 1989–1993 period.

Reducing Government Expenditures. Another way to finance new spending on long-term care is through corresponding reductions in other government expenditures. In my view, the arena in which to begin the search for further expenditure reductions at this juncture is discretionary economic development and assistance programs. This includes federal programs that subsidize transportation (mass transit

and Amtrak); economic development activities (Economic Development Administration and Urban Development Action Grants); agri-
cultural subsidies; community development programs; and Defense
Department impact aid to public schools. It would also be possible to
raise beneficiary contributions to Medicare's acute care services in
order to help finance government coverage of long-term care. Other
observers would single out different areas of the budget for cutbacks,
such as national defense. The point here is not to develop a list of
specific cuts, but rather to indicate that cutting back other federal
expenditures by an equivalent amount is one way to finance a greater
measure of protection for catastrophic expenses under Medicare.

This option opens up the possibility of revisiting the federalism
debate and sorting the social functions judged appropriate for government into national, state, and local responsibilities. Senator Daniel
Evans and former Governor Charles Robb proposed a trade-off. It
entailed devolving to the states various federal community and economic development responsibilities in return for a greater federal role
in long-term care and a federal floor on public assistance benefits.

Summary and Conclusion

This chapter has suggested the need for fundamentally overhauling
the Medicare and Medicaid programs to increase their fairness, their
balance, and their ability to complement and even advance the
important role played by private financing mechanisms. Medicare
and Medicaid coverage has been heavily biased toward acute and
institutional care, leading to a combination of large and growing
public sector costs and simultaneous unmet needs.

The elderly and younger taxpayers spend a lot of money for
these programs, and yet the elderly remain vulnerable to financial
catastrophe. Rebalancing these programs not only would make sense
in its own right, but also would invigorate the market for private
insurance for long-term care and foster a public-private partnership
built on the idea of comparative advantage.

Some of these proposals will cost the government money, and
an effort has been made to provide some preliminary cost estimates.
Several options for fully financing the new commitments have also
been presented.

Much of the debate about how to finance long-term care has
involved abstract arguments over whether the federal government
should fund this care through a new program or the private sector
should provide the financing. In my view, there is a need for both
public and private financing. We have a public-private mixture now.

120

But the public sector provides a welfare net, while the private sector funding is largely out-of-pocket outlays that place an enormous burden on families. Thus, our payment system now is a blend of welfare and "victim payment." By redesigning the public commitment, we can achieve a better public-private combination that spreads the cost of care broadly and equitably across society. A mixture of public and private insurance would protect people from huge losses and still encourage them to obtain private protection for more typical or average outlays.

Notes

1. Corbin Liu, Kenneth Manton, and Barbara Marzetta Liu, "Home Care Expenses for the Disabled Elderly," *Health Care Financing Review*, vol. 7, no. 2 (Winter 1985), pp. 51–58.

2. Kathryn Langwell et al., "Early Experience of Health Maintenance Organizations under Medicare Competition Demonstrations," *Health Care Financing Review*, vol. 8, no. 3 (Spring 1987), pp. 37–55.

3. United Hospital Fund of New York, March 1987.

4. Committee on Ways and Means, U.S. House of Representatives, *Background Material and Data on Programs within the Jurisdiction of the Committee on Ways and Means*, 1987 Edition, March 6, 1987, p. 199.

5. Sheila R. Zedlewski and Jack A. Meyer, *Toward Ending Poverty among the Elderly and Disabled: Policy and Financing Options* (Washington, D.C.: Urban Institute Press, 1987).

6. Joshua Weiner et al., "Catastrophic Long-Term Care Insurance: A Public/Private Partnership," Paper prepared for the U.S. Department of Health and Human Services Task Force on Long-Term Health Care Policies, May 1987.

7. Congressional Budget Office, *Reducing the Deficit: Spending and Revenue Options*, 1988 Annual Report, March 1988, p. 325.

8. Ibid.

9. Ibid., p. 122.

10. Ibid., p. 125.

11. Zedlewski and Meyer, *Toward Ending Poverty*, p. 83.

12. Congressional Budget Office, *Reducing the Deficit*, p. 310.

8

Matching Policies for Retirement Years with Changing Demographic and Economic Conditions

Jack A. Meyer

The purpose of this chapter is to explore ways to tailor our retirement and health care policies to changing demographic and economic conditions. Its theme is the growing mismatch between our public and private sector policies toward retirement and health care and the objective conditions of the elderly population.

Everywhere one looks our retirement policies seem out of date. They encourage early retirement, that is, before age sixty-five, when by all accounts most Americans in their sixties are healthier today than ever before. Americans are also living longer, so that policies encouraging early retirement are helping to produce an unhealthy side effect of an otherwise favorable social development—a retired population whose retirement years almost equal its working years, with retirement generally meaning inactivity. This is unhealthy for the retired, who face growing boredom and loss of a sense of social contribution. And it is unhealthy for society, as funding public and private retirement programs for a swelling retired population imposes an increasing burden on a working population that will soon stop growing and may actually decline in size.

A second problem is that government health and retirement benefits do not adequately reflect the heterogeneous economic conditions of the elderly. Benefits go to wealthy dowagers and poor elderly widows on a similar basis, despite the obvious difference in their needs. Beneath the aggregate statistics on the well-being of the elderly, one can find poverty amid plenty and hardship amid comfort. What we lack is a fair system for recycling to the neediest older Americans some of the benefits paid out under retirement programs—for example, by taxing more of the benefits going to the better-off elderly.

A third aspect of the growing disparity between policy and need is the continuing bias in our health care policies toward acute care medicine, when the needs of our population are continuing to change in the direction of requiring more long-term care for chronic illness and disability. Health care reimbursement—public and private—is still based on the physician-directed medical model that made sense for the elderly thirty years ago but makes less sense today and will make no sense tomorrow. This imbalance is treated in more detail in another chapter in this volume, "Reforming Medicare and Medicaid."

A final problem is the strong bias in our health care and retirement policies toward helping the "young old" while neglecting the needs of the "old old." There is every indication that the young old as a group are better able to take care of themselves, physically and financially, than ever before while the old old are increasingly in need of assistance.

In summary, our health care and retirement policies are uniform, but the population is diverse. These policies encourage people not to work, when they are more able to work than ever before. They pay for complex and heroic health care intervention nearly in full for all income groups but offer straightforward assistance with the activities of daily living only after families are pauperized. They favor the young old, who are the least needy of the elderly.

These policies are out of line with changing demographics and improved health because they are based on an anachronistic image of a sixty-five-year-old person as dependent and needy. Some sixty-five-year-olds are dependent, but most are not or need not be if we create the right incentives. Our policies are also increasingly out of line with the rapidly changing requirements of our economy. They work against achieving two important economic goals—increasing our pathetically low rate of private saving and capitalizing on the experience and skills of older workers in an increasingly tight labor market. In short, our policies often discourage younger Americans from saving and older Americans from working.

This chapter examines these mismatches and disjunctures in our policies and offers a broad agenda for reform to help tailor them to new demographic and economic realities.

The Changing Conditions of the Elderly

Recent long-range estimates of the incomes and assets of the elderly illustrate two important points. First, as a group they will be getting wealthier. Our policies should recognize this and stop overcompensating higher-income older citizens with generous public benefits. Second, lurking beneath the averages that show rising income and wealth are pockets of hardship and deprivation. Our policies should also recognize this hardship, which is masked by composite portraits of the elderly.

A recent study by the Brookings Institution projects that the median family income of the roughly 31 million Americans sixty-five and older in the period from 1986 to 1990 will be $9,314. It will then nearly double, in real terms, to $17,210 in the years from 2016 to 2020 for the estimated 50 million people who will then be in that age group. The assets of the elderly are also expected to increase in real terms over this period, from a median of $59,230 in 1986–1990 to $79,050 in 2016–2020—suggesting that the developments of the late 1970s and early 1980s documented in the chapter by John Weicher can be expected to continue well into the future.[1]

These aggregate figures, however, hide important problems facing certain subgroups of older Americans. For example, those eighty-five and older are projected to have a median family income of only $8,000 in 1987 dollars, in the period from 2016 to 2020, compared with $23,200 for those sixty-five to seventy-four years old. Those eighty-five and older also have only one-third the financial assets of those sixty-five to seventy-four, although the value of their home equity is more nearly comparable.[2] Thus the older elderly are not poor in total assets but hold a high proportion of their wealth in illiquid form, making it difficult to meet expenses for unreimbursed acute and long-term health care.

The Haves and the Have-Nots

The United States has a much better social protection system for a substantial portion of the labor force than it had half a century ago. This system provides workers with income when they cannot work because of old age, disability, ill health, or unemployment through a combination of a rapidly maturing public social insurance system and a corresponding private system that relies mainly on employer-provided benefits.

Under our mixed public-private social insurance system, this protection is earned by workers. They make contributions to public programs through a payroll tax. Employers also pay their share of these taxes, and many contribute as well to private pension, health insurance, and disability insurance plans on behalf of their employees.

In addition to our work-based social insurance system, we have a welfare-based public assistance system providing a combination of cash assistance and in-kind benefits on a means-tested basis. The in-kind benefits are provided through such programs as Medicaid and

125

food stamps. This protection is decidedly and purposefully less generous than the protection provided through social insurance.

The problem is that many Americans are not participating in our increasingly generous work-based social protection systems and will never secure adequate protection for old age through the fallback welfare system. These people are not as well protected as those in the work-related system during their working years and are also failing to build credits for their retirement. Consequently, when we compare the resources of the elderly with the likely expenses they will face in retirement years, we find that many Americans today can take care of themselves while many others are badly in need of assistance. For the former group a quiet revolution has occurred since the dark days of the Great Depression; for the latter it is as if they were back in the 1930s.

Thus the challenge facing public policy today is how better to target aid to those who have been left out of the public-private social protection system. This requires recognizing both the greater ability of many people to provide for their own health and retirement income needs and the corresponding need to help those who are not earning benefits, either because they are not working or because their jobs do not confer the kind of protection that many other workers enjoy. This effort will involve both recycling and retargeting public assistance in the direction of need, as well as expanding the private social protection system in areas where it is weak.

Pension Coverage: The Haves and the Have-Nots

About half the workers in the private sector today have employer-provided pension plans. Over the past half-century, a huge growth has taken place in these plans, paralleling the enormous growth and gradual maturation of the social security system. Private pension coverage has edged downward in the 1980s, however; the Employee Benefit Research Institute (EBRI) estimated that 48 percent of workers were participating in such plans in 1985, down from a peak of 56 percent in 1979.[3] But the proportion of today's work force that has coverage is still much higher than the proportion of retired persons that receives pension benefits. Thus relatively more retirees will be receiving such benefits in the coming years.

The EBRI projects another increase in private pension coverage in the future. It forecasts that 63 percent of workers who were thirty-three to forty-two years old in 1987 will have employer-sponsored pension coverage when they retire.[4] This projection, however, assumes no change in the proportion of workers covered within individual industries; it is based on projected shifts in employment among industries. It seems fair to say, therefore, that we are uncertain whether private pension coverage will expand.

Pension coverage is much less extensive in the private sector than among government workers (48 percent versus 87 percent for federal workers and 82 percent for state and local employees in 1983). Coverage is higher in both sectors among members of the so-called ERISA work force, defined as those who meet the standards of the Employee Retirement Income Security Act (ERISA) for plan participation (that is, are between twenty-five and sixty-four years old, work at least 1,000 hours per year, and have at least one year of service). Among this group 65 percent of private sector employees and 88 percent of government employees were covered by pensions in 1983.

There is also an important distinction between participating in an employer-provided pension plan at some time during the working years and actually being entitled to future benefits under such a plan. For example, only 31 percent of the private sector ERISA work force and 57 percent of government workers in 1983 were entitled to future benefits.[5] Participating in a pension plan does not ensure entitlement to benefits. Although pension portability has improved since the enactment of ERISA, in some circumstances workers still lose their rights to future pension benefits when they change jobs.

The spread of employee pensions has augmented total private saving in the United States. Americans save much less than citizens of other industrial countries, but total personal savings in the United States would be even less were it not for the expansion of private pension plans. The growth of pensions has reduced the pressure to raise payroll taxes even further and rely exclusively on social security to ensure a minimum retirement income.

In recent years individual retirement accounts (IRAs), Keogh plans, and 401k salary reduction plans have also expanded. It is a little early to tell how the 1986 tax reform legislation will affect participation in these plans. This legislation limited the tax preferences associated with IRAs, but it seems plausible that they will continue to be purchased by middle- and upper-income households.

With IRAs, Keogh plans, 401ks, and other savings instruments, working people have many ways to put some money aside for their retirement years and receive tax deferments for doing so. An important determinant of financial security for the elderly is whether they are able to supplement social security with pension income or earnings from work.

In 1984 elderly couples in the upper quintile of the income distribution (that is, with $30,100 or more of annual income) were

127

nearly six times as likely to have income from government pensions and more than twice as likely to have income from private pensions as elderly couples in the lowest quintile (with less than $10,100 of annual income). Among elderly individuals the differences were even greater. Those in the highest quintile ($13,700 or more) were 18.5 times as likely as those in the lowest quintile (less than $4,200) to have government pensions and 12.5 times as likely to have private pensions.[6]

In addition, about half the elderly individuals in the upper quintile and fewer than 5 percent of those in the two lowest quintiles (with annual incomes below $5,800) had income from assets other than pensions. Indeed, elderly individuals in the lowest quintile received 75 percent of their income from social security and 18 percent from means-tested cash transfers such as Supplemental Security Income (SSI). In contrast, individuals in the upper quintile received 22 percent of their income from assets and none from means-tested transfers.

A fourth of the upper-quintile couples but only 2 percent of couples in the lowest quintile and 6 percent of those in the next lowest quintile had income from earnings.[7] This comparison should heighten our concern about disincentives to work during the preretirement or early retirement years.

The Forgotten Elderly

Although pension coverage among the elderly is growing, a group chiefly in the low- to moderate-income range falls into the cracks between government programs for the elderly poor and the employer-based private pension system. This private system takes a lot of pressure off the government (which is presumably why the government provides it with tax preferences), but it by no means covers everyone. Those who are not participating in it cannot be presumed to fall under the protection of public programs even if they are poor— and particularly if they are only near poor.

Although low- to moderate-income workers do participate in pension plans and invest in IRAs, their participation and coverage are lower, and their vulnerability is therefore greater. For example, in 1983 only 32 percent of nonfarm wage and salary workers who earned less than $10,000 annually were covered by pension plans; the figures were 68 percent for those who earned between $10,000 and $25,000 and 82 percent for those who earned $25,000 or more.[8] Similarly, 36 percent of those who earned $10,000–15,000 in 1982 and were eligible to contribute to IRAs or spousal IRAs did so; the corresponding figure for those earning $15,000–20,000 was 49 percent and for those earning over $50,000, 77 percent.[9]

Workers who do have private pensions will see the value of their benefits decline in real terms during their retirement years because, unlike social security, such benefits are not usually indexed to inflation. Most pensions pay a fixed dollar amount based on peak earnings (for example, a percentage of average earnings during the five highest-salaried years). This is an aspect of the mismatch between policies and needs: the needs of the elderly for income may increase during old age as they experience more health problems and are likelier to require long-term care—yet their real incomes tend to decline. The vulnerability of the old old thus increases, and the bias in our payment policies toward acute medical care rather than long-term chronic care increases it further. As people age, then, their private pension income usually shrinks in real terms while their need for health care is less likely to be met by insurance.

The elderly seem to be sorting themselves into haves and have-nots with respect to pensions. The haves may grow as a share of the total in the next decade or two, as the effect of the spread of pensions in past years is felt when some of these workers retire. The growth in relative numbers of pension recipients is expected to taper off, however, leaving a substantial number of retired persons without such benefits.

Health Care Benefits for the Elderly—A Similar Story

A similar polarization of the elderly into haves and have-nots can be observed in health care. About two-thirds of the elderly have private supplementary health insurance, or medigap policies, covering various cost-sharing obligations imposed by Medicare. About 22 percent have company-paid retirement health benefits (usually these people also have private supplementary insurance policies and thus have three sources of protection). Yet in 1985 about 21 percent of the elderly had neither private supplementary health insurance nor eligibility for Medicaid. It is particularly distressing that among the elderly with incomes below $5,000 (who are clearly poor and most in need of help in meeting Medicare's cost-sharing requirements), 29 percent had neither private coverage nor Medicaid.[10]

Most of the elderly poor who get SSI are also eligible for Medicaid. But only about half the elderly poor who are eligible for SSI actually receive it, and some of the poor are not even eligible because the income cutoff line for SSI eligibility is below the federal poverty line. As a result of these factors tying Medicaid to welfare, *only a little over a third of the elderly poor get Medicaid benefits.*

States have several options in qualifying the elderly for Medicaid. They can automatically provide it to SSI recipients, they can require SSI recipients to file separate applications for eligibility (with no additional requirements), or they can impose more restrictive income and resource standards and more restrictive definitions of blindness and disability than those used in the SSI program.

Thirty states now provide automatic coverage, six require an additional application, and fourteen have more restrictive eligibility standards. In addition, Medicaid's covered services vary from state to state; for example, some states cover prescription drugs and optometry services, and others do not. Thirty-five states offer Medicaid benefits to those eligible only for SSI state supplements (not the federal payment), and twenty-nine states offer "medically needy" programs to persons who cannot qualify for SSI benefits because their incomes or resources are a little too high but who have unusually large medical bills. Thus some elderly poor are worse off than others in receiving public assistance for health care simply because of where they live.

A New Policy Strategy for Helping the Have-Nots

A stalemate has developed over how to deal with those who have been left out of the social protection system that we have built for most of our older citizens. On one side are unrealistic calls for mandated health and pension benefits for all jobs. Such proposals would lead many workers to lose their jobs altogether and limit opportunities for workers entering the labor force. They treat all jobs alike and would load the same mandates on a part-time or temporary job as on permanent work and require benefits even for workers covered under the pension or health plan of another member of the household.

On the other side are those who believe that nothing should be done and that the current system is fine. They point to the progress we have made for a large chunk of our work force and retired workers and ignore the plight of those who have not shared in that progress.

The challenge is to deal with the have-nots in the labor force— who will be tomorrow's needy elderly—in a way that does not hamstring our economy and that preserves the flexibility in our labor force that is vital to the competitive position of U.S. firms in world markets. That is, the challenge is to enhance the capacity of U.S. business to provide a more complete social protection system. This is preferable to establishing a wholly public social protection system or

130

to imposing rigid mandates on business that disregard the ability to finance such an expanded benefit package. But if this challenge is met by changing public policies, business must respond by providing broader coverage and not duck the issue.

A series of new benefit mandates—for pensions, health care, pregnancy leave, and so on—will translate into either downward pressure on wages or higher unemployment unless something is done to put business in a better position to afford these benefits. Given the downward rigidity of wages, the most probable result of universal mandates would be higher unemployment. This unemployment results not only from layoffs but also from jobs never created that would have been under more flexible wage and benefit policies.

Rather than adopting policies that reduce business earnings and take new benefits from one group of workers who remain employed out of the hides of another group who lose their jobs, we should try to bolster productivity, lower unit labor costs, increase saving and investment, and expand output. This would enable us in time to extend benefits by creating the real resources to do so, instead of moving resources around a fixed-size board in a zero-sum game.

We are not making the sacrifices in current consumption needed to expand the economic pie and earn new benefits under a private sector social protection system, as is evident from the following comparisons. From the mid-1960s to the mid-1970s Japan's rate of capital investment in manufacturing exceeded that of the United States by a factor of four.[11] Americans must save more and devote more of their savings to investment in new plant and equipment rather than to consumer goods if we are to match the performance of our trading partners and competitors. Personal saving, however, is at a historic low in the United States, averaging 3 to 4 percent of GNP over the 1985–1987 period, below our more usual range of 5 to 9 percent of GNP, which itself is low by international standards.

The low rate of consumer saving is made worse by the fact that our government is not undertaking its own needed belt tightening. The federal government's profligacy is manifest in the continuing huge annual federal deficits and a stock of federal debt that reached $2.6 trillion in 1988. Annual deficits are somewhat smaller now as a percentage of our GNP. But further progress is required. Moreover, the United States—the world's largest creditor nation for most of this century—is now the largest debtor nation. We owe an estimated $400 billion to the rest of the world and are increasingly beholden to their willingness to extend us further credit.

The fall 1987 budget compromise between the administration and the Congress is a classic example of going through the motions of belt tightening without actually moving the belt buckle. This package was replete with phony savings and postponements of expenditures instead of real long-range savings that would reflect a change in the growth path of entitlement programs that are not well targeted to vital human needs.

Thus a sensible long-term path to enabling (rather than requiring) U.S. industry to provide more extensive employee benefits and, therefore, better protection for the expenses of old age, would include the following kinds of measures: (1) stimulating private saving and thereby enhancing our ability to invest in new plant, equipment, and technology; (2) reducing government dissaving, which would have a similar favorable effect by freeing up the pool of private saving, however large it is, for investment; (3) accelerating steps under way in the private sector to reduce wasteful expenditures on health care and thus achieve given health care objectives with fewer real resources; (4) increasing the commitment by business to use some of the additional profits emerging from these strategies to provide better social protection and job security to workers; and (5) relying more on flexible compensation, gain-sharing pay arrangements, and modernized work rules that heighten workers' interest in improved productivity and increase the flexibility of our labor force. If workers cooperate in these efforts, they will have earned a right to better job security and better benefits.

Changing Public Policy toward Health Care

The discussion so far has centered on private sector responsibility for extending employee benefits to augment protection for workers when they retire. We also need to revise public policies to recycle some of the vast sums of money flowing into social insurance trust funds to those elderly people who are impoverished and receiving inadequate public assistance. The chapter entitled "Reforming Medicare and Medicaid" offers a detailed strategy for meeting some of the income and health care needs of low-income older citizens, along with a menu of financing options.

To summarize that strategy briefly, we should uncouple Medicaid from welfare-related cash assistance and extend it to a greater proportion of the low-income elderly, irrespective of their participation in the SSI program. This would enable more low-income elderly persons to receive public assistance for the substantial copayments and deductibles associated with Medicare. We should also increase the personal needs allowance under Medicaid. The recently enacted catastrophic health care legislation takes important steps in this direction.

Although it is important to offer Medicaid to the poor who are not receiving SSI benefits, we should get to the heart of the problem by relaxing the overrestrictive SSI asset criteria for eligibility and raising SSI benefits, particularly for single persons, who now receive a maximum of only three-fourths of the federal poverty-level income even if they have no other income. Most do have some other income from social security, but an estimated 20 percent of the elderly do not receive social security benefits; it is this group, particularly elderly widows living alone, that raises concern about the need for a higher maximum SSI benefit.

We should also use targeted government subsidies to assist households with the purchase of private long-term care insurance. This public assistance might take the form of either premium subsidies or stop-loss and reinsurance protection.

The financing options presented in the chapter on Medicare and Medicaid would generate sufficient revenue to take these steps in a fiscally responsible fashion.

Changing Retirement Policy to Encourage Work

The decision about when to quit working is a personal one, based on health, alternative uses of time, and family resources. Work is not for all older people—some may be ill or disabled; others may be burned out from years of hard work.

For people in their sixties and early seventies, however, we have stacked the deck against the option of working, and this could be changed. Changing demographic and economic circumstances also make it more important than ever that we alter our policies to encourage rather than discourage work among the healthy young old. In the increasingly tight labor markets expected in the future, more effective use of experienced older workers is not only a desirable social goal but also a way to help achieve our economic objectives. Indeed, at some future time when the work force begins to decline slightly while the elderly population increases sharply, generating job opportunities for older workers—and creating the incentives for them to seize such opportunities—may become an economic imperative.

In their chapter in this volume, Wayne and Susan Vroman document the startling decline in labor force participation among men in their late fifties and early sixties. Noting that the proportion of men in these age groups who were not working at all tripled between 1954 and 1984, they conclude that the rise is unlikely to be explained by health. The health of older men as a group has not deteriorated and may have improved over this period.

Research evidence suggests that the early retirement provisions of both social security and private pension plans have been important, perhaps key, factors in fostering early retirement.[12] In recent years Congress has taken some steps to reduce the incentive to retire early that was built into the social security program. For example, the 1986 tax reform legislation required a full actuarial reduction in the defined benefit amount received by workers retiring before the normal retirement age of sixty-five. The old law had stipulated such a reduction only for people retiring at age sixty-two or earlier.

Further steps could be taken, including the controversial measure of lowering the proportion of full benefits (now 80 percent) that a person who takes early retirement may receive, as proposed by President Reagan and resoundingly rejected by Congress in 1981. The Social Security Amendments of 1983 did contain provisions that will gradually raise the age of eligibility for full benefits from sixty-five to sixty-seven during the period from 2000 to 2022. The age at which early retirement can be taken under social security is also scheduled to rise from sixty-two to sixty-five over this period.

As business grapples with the issue of incentives for older workers, it will face conflicting pressures. On one side will be a temptation to encourage them to retire early, making way for lower-paid younger workers who are also more recently educated and trained. On the other side, as time goes on, firms will find the supply of new entrants more limited, and the competition for younger workers will become more intense. In addition, companies may find that they are being penny-wise and pound-foolish to encourage experienced, skilled personnel to resign in favor of cheaper but greener workers.

Many factors will enter such calculations, including pay scales, pension obligations, health care costs for retired employees, and productivity. Employers should consider tailoring jobs to the special needs—and potential contributions—of older workers. Through part-time or part-year work and revised or scaled-down job responsibilities, some older workers can enter a kind of "step-down" position that is quite different from stepping out of the work force altogether. For executives in their early sixties, business may want to consider new alternatives somewhere between continuing in a regular management position and receiving the "golden handshake" or the gold watch.

Concluding Thoughts

A new strategy is needed to improve the match between the policies that govern the work and retirement system and changing demographic trends and economic requirements. We need to bolster productivity, introduce more flexible compensation, and foster economic growth to enhance the capacity of our private sector to extend its employer-based social protection system to the uncovered members of the work force. This is preferable to imposing rigid government mandates as a strategy to help tomorrow's retired persons meet their health care and other needs.

We also need stronger incentives for workers to save and for business to invest. Along with corresponding measures that bring our federal deficit under control, such steps will arrest the dangerous inclination to stretch out a consumption binge during which we have been living beyond our means—and to leave it to our children to come to the rescue when we cannot meet our own needs.

We must also recycle to our neediest older citizens some of the lightly taxed benefits paid to people of all incomes under public social insurance programs. We must reverse the current practice of providing the most generous benefits to the better-off young elderly and give more help to the old old. Taxing social security as we tax private pensions, for example, would provide a growing pool of funds that could be earmarked for the unmet health care, housing, and other needs of the elderly poor.

We need to change the incentives in our pension programs—public and private—that discourage older Americans from working. If this step is combined with serious efforts by employers to redesign jobs to fit the needs and capabilities of older workers, we can harness their skills and experience. As we move toward an older society, such measures will help us stretch available resources and target them to costly unmet needs—including long-term care and a decent minimum living standard for all our elderly citizens.

Notes

1. Alice M. Rivlin and Joshua M. Weiner, *Caring for the Disabled Elderly: Who Will Pay?* (Washington, D.C.: Brookings Institution, 1988), p. 10.

2. Ibid.

3. Employee Benefit Research Institute, *America in Transition: Benefits for the Future* (Washington, D.C.: EBRI, 1987), p. 37.

4. Ibid., p. 38.

5. Emily S. Andrews, *The Changing Profile of Pensions in America* (Washington, D.C.: EBRI, 1985), p. 16.

6. Nancy Gordon, "Statements on the Elderly and Health Care Expenditures," before the Subcommittee on Health and the Environment, Committee on Energy and Commerce, U.S. House of Representatives, Congressional Budget Office, March 26, 1986, mimeo.

7. Ibid.

8. Andrews, *Changing Profile*, pp. 51–58.

9. Ibid., p. 81.

10. U.S. House of Representatives, Committee on Ways and Means, *Background Material and Data on Programs within the Jurisdiction of the Committee on Ways and Means*, 1987 ed., March 6, 1987, p. 199.

11. Kenneth McLennan, "Global Competition and the Special Challenges of Developing Countries: A U.S. Perspective" (Paper prepared for the National Science Foundation Conference on Cooperation and Competition in the Global Economy, April 27–29, 1986), p. 15.

12. Gary S. Fields and Olivia S. Mitchell, *Retirement, Pensions, and Social Security* (Cambridge, Mass.: MIT Press, 1984).

9

Can the Elderly Afford Long-Term Care?

Marilyn Moon and Timothy M. Smeeding

Can the elderly afford long-term care? As to many questions, the answer is, "It depends."

The high-income elderly can afford to pay for long-term care themselves, and the poorest can rely on Medicaid coverage. But a significant group of lower-middle-income elderly find it difficult to afford such care and painful to spend down to eligibility for Medicaid. Long-term care becomes affordable to more elderly people, however, when the risks are spread across the population through private insurance. Moreover, if coverage is purchased early enough—for example, when people are in their fifties—even those with modest incomes can afford it. Private long-term-care coverage cannot yet be considered a viable option, however. Such insurance is neither readily available nor in great demand. Because current plans limit the services covered, they do not truly protect the elderly from financial catastrophe.

This chapter assesses the ability of today's elderly and of future cohorts to pay for long-term care. The ability to pay for such care—directly or through insurance—is measured in relation to current and expected future income and wealth. Private long-term-care insurance and alternative sources of support are discussed as optional ways to pay indirectly for such care.

We briefly discuss possible policy options for financing long-term care and the trade-offs among them at the end of the chapter. We suggest that both increased private insurance and expansion of the public-sector safety net might lead to adverse side effects. Stimulating the growth of private insurance—for example, through public tax subsidies—would benefit the rich more than the middle class. Ex-

The authors would like to thank Enrique Lamas and Christine Ross for providing unpublished data. Jack Meyer offered helpful comments on an earlier draft of this paper. We hold our institutions and sponsors harmless with respect to the contents of this paper and its conclusions.

tending Medicaid benefits (or combined Medicare-Medicaid benefits) to the lower-middle-income elderly would discourage many with modest incomes from buying private insurance. These side effects should be weighed against the advantages of public and private strategies for expanding coverage of long-term care. Options for helping the lower-middle-income elderly, particularly the oldest among them, pose the toughest challenges and require careful consideration by future policy makers.

The Income and Wealth of the Elderly

Today's Elderly. The income and wealth of the elderly have improved greatly over the past two decades. In the mid-1960s nearly 30 percent of older Americans had incomes below the federal poverty line; today only about one of eight is poor. Moreover, the per capita income of the average elderly household has caught up with the average for the nonelderly, and the wealth of the elderly has increased markedly over the past decade, as the chapter by John Weicher documents.

A few words of caution about these generalizations are appropriate, however. First, an examination of the income distribution of the elderly reveals a large group of near poor; indeed, about one of five older Americans has an income below 125 percent of the poverty line. Second, middle-income elderly are highly vulnerable to the potentially huge expenses of long-term care and can be impoverished quickly by expenses that fall outside the coverage of Medicare or private health insurance. Third, in recent years some tax preferences for the elderly have been scaled back. These changes have reduced the resources available for long-term care. Finally, the increases in average incomes mask the slower rise experienced by groups of the elderly—since the average rises with new entrants into the population over sixty-five, who are better off than their elders. With these caveats in mind, however, we can conclude that rising social security benefits and Medicare have substantially improved the economic well-being of older Americans over the past two decades.

Tomorrow's Elderly: The Good Times Generation. Recent evidence from the 1950 to 1980 censuses and from wealth surveys taken between 1962 and 1984 suggests that the next generation of the elderly—those born between 1925 and 1935, who will reach sixty-five between 1990 and 2000—will be better off than today's elderly.[1] These people (aged thirty to forty in 1965) have had the good fortune to be in their prime working years during the period of maximum earnings growth of the halcyon 1960s. The value of their homes soared during the inflationary 1970s, and their financial assets were liquid enough to enable them to take advantage of the high real interest rates and stock market boom of the early to middle 1980s. Indeed, people born in the 1930s have been dubbed the "good times" generation by demographer Carl Harter.

A Federal Reserve Board survey of consumer finances found that the mean net worth of those fifty-five to sixty-four in 1983 was 84 percent above the national mean net worth.[2] Similar surveys for 1962 and 1969 found that the fifty-five- to sixty-four-year-olds in those years (whose survivors are among today's elderly) had net worth holdings ranging from 39 to 56 percent above the average. In 1983 the mean net worth of those forty-five to fifty-four was 41 percent above the national mean. But a similar age group two decades earlier (1960s) had a net worth only 3 to 7 percent above the national average.

This generation is also more likely to have a greater share of persons receiving higher private pensions and, because of their high earnings, larger social security benefits than any preceding generation. These average indicators suggest—even assuming that the stock market boom of the mid-1980s will not continue into the next decade—that tomorrow's elderly will be better off than today's.

Looking beneath the Averages

Despite the rosy overall picture painted by the evidence cited, the heterogeneity among the elderly is still troublesome. About one of five older Americans lives on an income below 125 percent of the poverty line, and the concentration of the near-poor group with incomes between 100 and 125 percent of the poverty line is greater for the elderly than for the nonelderly.

Moreover, these poorer elderly persons have not gained in recent years at the same pace as their higher-income counterparts. Incomes have grown more slowly for the elderly at the bottom of the income distribution than for those at the top.[3] Thus the average growth in incomes of the elderly overstates the gains being made by those who start out with lower incomes.

The elderly with the lowest incomes are also likely to be most at risk for long-term care. The oldest of the old are more likely to be poor, and their incomes are substantially below those of the elderly in their late sixties or early seventies.[4] To some extent this reflects cohort differences that will improve over time. But these more limited resources also result from the large number of the oldest old who live alone. In particular, women living alone dominate the group age eighty and older—and it is precisely these elderly persons who are most likely to be institutionalized.

Since our concern is not just with the income of the elderly but also with their ability to afford to insure themselves for health care expenditures (for both acute and long-term care), the group at risk extends beyond the poor and the near poor. In fact, many of the poor can rely on Medicaid in case of major illness, particularly one requiring institutionalization. If they have few or no assets, they should be covered when the need arises. It is the next group up the income ladder, the lower-middle-income elderly, who face the greatest challenge in protecting themselves against the costs of long-term care.

Several researchers have indicated that a large proportion of lower-middle-income elderly persons are and will continue to be a source of concern, especially with regard to medical care and long-term and chronic care needs.[5] In particular, the elderly whose annual incomes are between the poverty line and two and a half times that level (roughly $6,000 to $15,000) are most likely to have little or no health insurance coverage to supplement Medicare. More than 25 percent of elderly Medicare enrollees with incomes below $15,000 in 1984 neither had private supplemental coverage nor were eligible for Medicaid, compared with only 10 percent of those whose incomes exceeded $25,000. Moreover, the proportion of persons without supplemental coverage rises with age and with poor health.[6] Within this group the third with the lowest incomes will probably qualify for Medicaid if a major illness strikes. Once they have reached this point (assuming they live in a state that covers the medically needy), they are unlikely to incur additional out-of-pocket costs for either acute or chronic long-term care. The rest, however, face a substantial risk of high and crippling expenses for acute-care needs alone.

The large number of this group who do not buy supplemental acute-care insurance are also unlikely to be able to purchase long-term-care insurance. For those in the lower-middle-income range who now purchase supplemental coverage, the additional expense of private long-term-care insurance might be prohibitive. If so, the unfortunate choice may come between long-term-care insurance and medigap. Perhaps as many as half the elderly in this income range would lack adequate combined insurance.

Before explicitly considering the affordability of private insurance for long-term care, however, we concentrate on the question of who can afford to pay out of pocket for such care. Private insurance is not yet an option for most older Americans. Even if it becomes more widely available, those already over sixty-five are unlikely to benefit immediately.

The variation in wealth among the elderly determines their ability to afford long-term care. Table 9–1 presents the joint distribution of income and wealth among the population sixty-five and older in 1984. Of most concern are the two bottom quartiles of the income distribution. The lowest 50 percent of households of all ages, which had incomes below $24,000 in 1984, included a disproportionate share of elderly households. The bottom quartile contained 43.7 percent of all units with a reference person sixty-five or older and 54.4 percent of those with a reference person seventy-five or older.[7] The mean total net worth of the lowest quartile of elderly households was roughly $40,000. If the average nursing home stay for this group is 456 days at a cost of about $50 per day, roughly $23,000 in assets would cover the cost. There are other considerations, such as differences in length of stay and in the number of persons in the household versus the number needing nursing home care. Nevertheless, it appears that on average even elderly people in this low-income group could cover their long-term-care needs directly by expending all their resources.

Once home equity is excluded from net worth, however, mean wealth drops to about $16,000—not enough to cover an average stay for one person. Moreover, such calculations assume that wealth is earmarked only to meet long-term-care needs. For many of the elderly, income from assets is an important source of the funds necessary to maintain a reasonable standard of living before, and sometimes after, a nursing home stay. But even these figures hide the variation within each quartile. Among all elderly households, for instance, median net worth was only about 60 percent of mean net worth in 1984.[8] Those with unusually high resources pull up the average and distort the picture of what a typical elderly household has at its command.

To consider the joint distribution of income and net worth in a way that enables us to focus on the middle-income elderly, we have employed data for 1979 provided by Radner and Vaughn in a 1986 study.[9] Table 9–2 shows the percentage distribution of elderly households in the first two census money-income quintiles (defined for all households) during 1979. These included 72.1 percent of all households with a reference person sixty-five or older and 77.7 percent of those with a reference person seventy-five or older. Higher-income elderly households—those with annual incomes of $12,849 or more, who were in the three top income quintiles—are assumed to be able to "afford" nursing home care.[10] Among those with incomes below

141

TABLE 9-1
Household Net Worth, by Age Group and Income Quartile, 1984

	Total Population	65+	65–69	70–74	75+
Number of households (thousands)	86,783	18,151	5,668	5,014	7,468
Mean household income (dollars)	26,868	17,534	22,426	17,264	14,002
		Distribution by Income Quartile (percent)			
Household income quartile					
Total	100.0	100.0	100.0	100.0	100.0
Less than $10,800	25.0	43.7	30.0	43.2	54.4
$10,800–23,999	25.0	36.7	42.8	38.5	30.9
$24,000–47,999	25.0	15.4	20.9	13.9	12.3
$48,000 or more	25.0	4.2	6.3	4.4	2.4

Mean Net Worth (dollars)

Household income quartile					
Total	96,406	102,770	123,851	96,823	88,371
Less than $10,800	27,858	40,731	39,896	30,047	41,978
$10,800–23,999	50,623	91,996	87,254	91,043	97,777
$24,000–47,999	77,125	184,562	172,594	187,131	198,010
$48,000 or more	230,018	553,301	615,486	517,742	470,364

Mean Net Worth Excluding Home Equity (dollars)

Household income quartile					
Total	58,498	62,875	79,220	59,412	52,795
Less than $10,800	11,770	16,489	15,902	15,086	17,483
$10,800–23,999	25,160	50,198	45,707	48,018	56,743
$24,000–47,999	40,237	124,012	114,245	120,293	139,381
$48,000 or more	156,824	441,290	496,374	408,190	369,841

SOURCES: Enrique J. Lamas and John M. McNeil, "Household Asset Ownership and Wealth Holding in 1984: Data from the Survey of Income and Program Participation" (Paper presented to the American Economic Association, New York, December 29, 1985); and unpublished tabulations courtesy of Enrique Lamas, U.S. Bureau of the Census.

TABLE 9-2

NET WORTH AND FINANCIAL ASSETS AMONG THE ELDERLY, 1979

	Wealth Range (dollars)	Households with Reference Person 65 or Older (percent)			
		65+	65–69	70–74	75+
Elderly in bottom two income quintiles		72.1	64.4	74.3	77.7
Net worth					
Bottom quintile	0–3,143	10.9	9.2	10.1	12.9
Next 2 quintiles	3,144–37,263	32.4	25.3	31.8	39.1
Top 2 quintiles	37,264+	28.8	29.9	32.4	25.7
Financial assets[a]					
Bottom 3 quintiles	0–3,310	39.2	37.2	39.0	41.4
4th quintile	3,311–15,248	16.2	10.4	18.4	19.6
Top quintile	15,249+	16.7	16.1	16.9	16.7

NOTE: Percentage of all households with a reference person sixty-five or over with money incomes below $12,849 in 1979.
a. Total net worth minus home equity, vehicles, and household durables.
SOURCE: D. Radner and D. Vaughn, "The Joint Distribution of Wealth and Income for Age Groups, 1979," in E. Wolff, ed., *International Comparisons of the Distribution of Household Wealth* (New York: New York University, 1986), tables 8, 10, 11.

$12,849, we look at ability to meet nursing home needs from two perspectives on wealth: net worth and financial assets (that is, net worth excluding vehicles, household durables, and home equity).

First, we assume that those with net worth of $3,143 or less—the lowest fifth of all households—would spend down and qualify for Medicaid to meet the average nursing home bill of about $17,000 in 1979.[11] Even if annual incomes are $10,000 or more, total resources and incomes are likely to be insufficient to meet nursing home bills. Presumably, this 10.9 percent of all elderly households and 12.9 percent of those with a reference person seventy-five or older would qualify for Medicaid if an average nursing home stay for one or more members arose.

Some of those with incomes below $12,849 can still afford long-term care because they have enough assets. For example, 28.8 percent of all elderly households in this lower-income group (and 25.7 percent with a reference person seventy-five or over) are in the top two asset quintiles. Their net worth totals $37,264 or more, and they are assumed to be able to afford nursing home care while still leaving some assets at death. Of greater concern is the 32.4 percent of households with a reference person sixty-five or over who have incomes below $12,849 and assets between $3,144 and $37,263. These households are at substantial risk of financial destitution if they have to pay for an average (or longer) nursing home stay for one or more members of the household.

Table 9–2 also shows financial assets only. The largest difference is the net equity in one's own home. All states will allow a spouse to exempt the home from countable assets under Medicaid if the other spouse needs nursing care. In most states the sale of a home is at the discretion of caseworkers where the money income and liquid assets of a single homeowner are insufficient to meet nursing home bills. The home may need to be sold to meet those bills. In an unknown number of cases, elderly persons with chronic health problems have transferred their homes to relatives to escape "capture" by Medicaid. In any case, excluding home equity provides a somewhat different look at the probability of financial devastation if a long nursing home stay arises.

We assume that the elderly with financial assets of $3,310 or less would qualify for Medicaid coverage of nursing home care if they *both* needed a long stay in a nursing home and could exclude home equity from their countable assets. In such cases 39.2 percent of the elderly with incomes below $12,849 would qualify for Medicaid. At the other end of the spectrum, 16.7 percent have sufficient liquid assets— $15,249 or more—to pay for the average nursing home stay with these funds alone. But about 16 percent of households with a reference person sixty-five or older and 20 percent of those with a reference person seventy-five or older would lose nearly all their financial assets if one person needed an average nursing home stay.[12]

Our data do not cover the number of elderly per household, the number needing long-term care, or the complicated state rules that govern treatment of home equity if nursing home care is needed. Nevertheless, we can roughly differentiate among those elderly who are likely to qualify for Medicaid, those who are likely to be able to afford an average long-term-care bill, and those of greatest concern— the lower- to middle-income and "middle-asset" elderly who risk financial devastation if faced with the average long-term-care bill. In this group we find 16 to 32 percent of all elderly households and about 20 to 39 percent of those most at risk of needing such care (the group with a reference person seventy-five or older). The number might also depend on whether the state in which the person lives has a program for the medically needy. In addition, a small proportion of people with higher incomes than considered here may have

145

no net worth. Without insurance they too would find it difficult to pay for long-term care.

Because the data in table 9–2 are for 1979, they do not capture the large increases in wealth realized by the elderly during the early 1980s. Moreover, we have not discussed the potential of home equity conversion plans that might allow the elderly to borrow on their homes to pay long-term-care bills. Still, these figures show that a substantial minority of the elderly will probably be unable to rely on the government or on their own finances to pay for nursing home care.

Long-Term Care: Need and Cost

The prospects of future long-term-care expenses impose a sobering mood on any discussion of the increasing well-being of the elderly. Despite improved longevity the need for long-term care is expected to remain fairly constant within age groups. Given the rapidly growing numbers of very old people, the stage is set for a dramatic rise in the demand for care. Further, the chances of finding new and less costly ways of delivering long-term care are slim. Even with the hoped-for innovations in case management and the delivery of services, which promise limited savings per case, meeting the medical and personal care needs of a "frail elderly" population will be costly.

The Need for Long-Term Care. The use of long-term care is highly concentrated among the oldest of the old. For example, although less than 2 percent of all women sixty-five to seventy-four have been institutionalized, one-fourth of those over eighty-five are in nursing homes. These figures are consistent with the incidence of functional limitations among the elderly. By age eighty-five nearly one-third of the elderly need assistance with personal care.[13]

Although the most dramatic increases in the proportion of the population over sixty-five are still in the future, the increases in the numbers of the oldest old, which reflect longer life spans, are already occurring. Moreover, these increases will become relatively more pronounced in the 1990s when fewer persons will turn sixty-five, reflecting the relatively low birthrate during the depression. Consequently, the average age of the elderly should rise substantially over the period.

Do these changes in the age distribution of the elderly imply growth in demand for care in the future? The answer rests with the likely changes in health status. In projecting the future needs of the elderly, some researchers have examined whether the factors leading to increased life expectancy also reduce the degree of functional limitation these older citizens face.[14] Although controversy persists over whether this group continues to be frail, the researchers conclude that the pattern of health status by age is likely to remain relatively unchanged. Consequently, they project a 53 percent increase in institutionalization for men and a 67 percent increase for women by the year 2000. But these figures probably underestimate the total increase in the demand for personal and medical care.

These projections are based on recent trends toward a slowing of the rate of institutionalization. Although several factors have undoubtedly contributed to this decline, one critical issue is whether more frail elderly persons are choosing to remain at home and receive care there. Home health services are a rapidly growing industry; and with continued high rates of support from families and friends, more people are finding it possible to avoid or at least delay entrance into nursing homes. Medicare expenditures for home health care have been growing at an annual rate of about 25 percent since 1977, largely reflecting greater use of services. The elderly can now be treated at home for conditions that once required hospitalization or institutionalization.

In addition, changes in public policy may substantially affect the use of services in the future. A number of states, for example, restrict the supply of nursing home beds to hold down Medicaid costs.[15] Relaxation of these limitations may result in rapid growth in capacity. The expansion of private insurance coverage or improved public provision of long-term care would exert pressures to allow increases in the supply of beds by increasing demand for services—although the increase would be concentrated in institutional services if coverage were improved only for them. In view of the preference of elderly persons for remaining at home whenever possible, however, insurers will face strong pressures to include home care options in their coverage. Thus we should expect rapid growth in the use of long-term care in the near future, some of which would be reflected in the costs of private insurance to individuals.

The Cost of Long-Term Care. Fortunately, the costs of long-term care are now rising more slowly than a few years ago. After increasing at an annual rate of about 16 percent from 1965 to 1980, nursing home costs grew only 11.2 percent annually in the first half of the 1980s. They are expected to rise less than 10 percent annually for the rest of the decade.[16]

The cost of an individual nursing home stay is more difficult to pin down because stays can vary enormously. Statistics from the 1977

National Nursing Home Survey provide some clues, however.[17] For all nursing home discharges (including the 12 percent of patients under sixty-five), the median stay was seventy-five days; about one-fourth of all discharged patients stayed for a year or more. Such figures substantially understate lengths of stay, however, since two of every five patients discharged went to another facility. Most often the transfer was to an acute-care hospital, after which the patient was likely to return to a nursing home.

The majority of patients discharged to their homes stayed less than three months; these short-term patients constitute about one-fifth of all discharges. In addition, 11.4 percent of discharges were patients who died within three months of admission. Thus nearly one-third of all nursing home discharges are short-stay patients (less than three months). Others have calculated the average length of stay for nursing home patients as 456 days.[18] The average period of institutionalization for the long-stay patients (more than three months) is 2.5 years. Long-stay patients in nursing homes face charges of $50 or more per day, or $20,000 to $30,000 per year. At least one-fourth of all nursing home patients remain a year or longer—and that number would be much greater if lengths of multiple, interrupted stays were known.

The rates of increase in the costs of home health care reflect both the rising costs of care and, more important, the change in the services provided.[19] Although increases in Medicare reimbursement rates have been limited in recent years to 6 percent or less for each category of care, the intensity of service use has been increasing. Consequently, growth in the average cost per visit is rising faster. Moreover, users of care have been receiving more of each kind of service.

The cost of a Medicare home health visit averaged $38 in 1983, less than the average reimbursement rate of $51 per day for skilled nursing care (which includes the costs of room and board). These home health costs, however, exclude such expenses as homemaker services, which are necessary to allow a functionally impaired person to remain at home. Cost thus becomes an issue in considering whether home health services will come to replace institutional care for some of the elderly. Any projection of future costs will have to take into account the kinds of services used.

Matching Need and Ability to Pay

To understand the degree to which the elderly can assume responsibility for meeting their own long-term-care needs, we need to explore two questions:

- What share of the resources of the elderly would have to be devoted to the cost of long-term-care insurance?
- What should we expect such persons to pay?

The first of these questions is factual. On the basis of the best projections, what share of income or assets would the elderly be required to spend to insure against potentially catastrophic long-term care needs? The second question raises several more subjective issues. At what age should people begin to purchase such insurance? What are reasonable premiums, given their resources? How likely are they to be willing to pay the share that decision makers judge "reasonable"? Before answering these questions, it is useful to look at current experience with private insurance.[20]

The Existing Market for Insurance. Much of this discussion must be based on conjecture, since markets for private long-term-care insurance are just developing. Only a few insurers offer such policies, and the policies generally provide conservative coverage. Insurers' experience with loss ratios is limited and offers few lessons for new initiatives.[21] Moreover, both the provisions and the premiums vary dramatically among plans, making cost comparisons difficult.

Insurers sometimes limit coverage by requiring a three-day prior hospitalization before coverage begins. This approach limits coverage to institutionalization that has a medical origin and avoids paying for custodial care. But for many of the very old, the need for long-term care is more likely to stem from a gradual deterioration in functional status than from a specific medical need. Private policies thus begin by limiting coverage for one of the major causes of institutionalization.

In addition, many policies explicitly exclude coverage for mental disease and disorders, again severely limiting the value of the policies to the elderly. Alzheimer's disease, which requires continuous care for many years, constitutes the ultimate fear for many. Policies that exclude mental disease, however, would preclude such coverage.

Current private policies often have a waiting period, which can substantially reduce the costs of insurance by eliminating from coverage the numerous patients with short-term needs. Such waiting periods may be desirable as a way of emphasizing catastrophic coverage, but they limit coverage for what may sometimes be expensive nursing care. At the other end of the time spectrum, most private policies also have a maximum length of coverage, usually three years. Thus they also do not provide catastrophic or "stop-loss" coverage.

Finally, most policies restrict acceptance of high-risk patients by asking questions about health, by limiting coverage for preexisting

149

conditions, and by reserving the right to deny renewal. These factors, together with the high cost of policies for persons first purchasing such insurance after the age of seventy or seventy-five, make it unlikely that private insurance will offer relief to those at risk in the short run. The most promising role for long-term-care insurance is to encourage those who are younger to plan ahead for their long-term-care needs and to consider purchasing private insurance as a supplement to their savings and income.

The Relative Costs of Long-Term-Care Insurance. Mark Meiners estimated that the 1981 costs of a prototype long-term-care insurance policy would have been $435 per year if offered to a sixty-five-year-old as part of a group policy.[22] If offered as an individual policy, the cost would have risen to $543. The expected annual benefits paid under such policies would have been $326—the actuarial value of coverage of $35 per day for a maximum of three years after a ninety-day waiting period.

Although Meiners tried to make generous assumptions about the use of services, he did not make any adjustments for demand induced by the insurance coverage. This latter point becomes particularly troublesome if coverage of home health care is included in private insurance, since such care can readily substitute for informal care. Consequently, in considering the costs of insurance in relation to incomes, we include an "upper-bound" estimate higher than the estimate for an individual insurance policy. Our estimates of the cost of insurance for sixty-five-year-olds thus range from $435 to $660 for 1981.

The cost of long-term-care insurance can be brought down substantially if policies are marketed to younger people. For example, premiums for the insurance recently offered by the American Association of Retired Persons (AARP) are age adjusted. Persons aged fifty to fifty-nine pay just 37 percent as much as those sixty-five to sixty-nine; sixty- to sixty-four-year-olds pay 63 percent as much.

To provide the reader with some idea of the costs of the prototypical Meiners policy for different age groups and family types, we deflated the costs of our prototypical individual policy from $435–610 in 1981 to $385–585 in 1979 using the nursing home price index; we then compared these costs with the 1979 pretax money incomes of three family types—couples, single men, and single women in various age groups (table 9–3). Both sets of estimates presented are based on the typical cost of an individual policy at ages sixty-five to sixty-nine, but the age ratings differ for the typical private policy and the AARP policy.

TABLE 9–3
PRIVATE LONG-TERM-CARE INSURANCE PREMIUMS AS A PERCENTAGE
OF AVERAGE MONEY INCOME, BY AGE GROUP AND FAMILY AND
POLICY TYPE, 1979

	50–54	55–59	60–64	65–69	70–74
Typical private policy					
Couple[a]	1.2–1.8	1.9–2.7	2.9–4.6	4.5–6.9	7.8–11.9
Single man	1.1–1.6	1.7–2.7	2.9–4.4	4.5–6.8	7.3–11.1
Single woman	1.6–2.4	2.5–3.8	3.9–5.9	5.4–8.3	8.8–13.4
AARP policy					
Couple[a]	1.1–1.6	1.1–1.7	2.2–3.4	4.5–6.9	8.6–14.4
Single man	1.0–1.5	1.1–1.6	2.1–3.3	4.5–6.8	8.0–12.3
Single woman	1.5–2.2	1.5–2.3	2.9–4.4	5.4–8.3	9.7–14.7
Age-specific Policy as a Percentage of 65–69 Policy					
Typical policy	0.40	0.60	0.84	1.00	1.48
AARP policy	0.37	0.37	0.63	1.00	1.63

NOTE: Both the typical policy and the AARP policy assume that the 1979 cost of the prototypal policy at ages sixty-five to sixty-nine as an individual policy would be $385 to $585.
a. Couples' policies are rated at twice the individual policy price.
SOURCES: *1980 Census of the Population,* unpublished data; "typical policy" age ratings derived from Mark Meiners, "The State of the Art in Long-Term Care Insurance," National Center for Health Services Research, 1984.

For all family types, private long-term-care insurance would have cost less than 2.5 percent of average money income if purchased at ages fifty to fifty-four. All the estimates in table 9–3 are based on mean incomes. Because of the skewed income distribution, medians may be better measures against which to compare costs. If the table were based on medians, which are about 80 percent of mean incomes for this age group, it would show premium costs still well under 3 percent of money income for this age group.[23]

One critical feature of private long-term-care insurance is the assumed constancy of the premium once a person enrolls. Many current policies offer a constant money premium after enrollment. But, of course, the later in life a person enrolls, the higher the premium. Moreover, as people age, their incomes fall. Thus although the typical policy was reasonably priced—at about 6 percent of income or less—until age sixty-four, it would have become expensive at average incomes beyond that age. For instance, the average sixty-five- to sixty-nine-year-old couple or single man would have paid 4.5

to 6.9 percent of income, and the average single woman would have paid 5.4 to 8.3 percent; the typical policy would have cost 7.8 to 13.4 percent of income for those seventy and older. If coverage is purchased early enough, then, it can be bought at a reasonable price. Waiting until retirement or later, however, makes the price prohibitive for the average elderly household. But early purchase also carries risks. If not indexed for inflation, benefits may be worth little in twenty or thirty years.

What Should the Elderly Be Expected to Pay? A substantial number of the elderly could afford some kind of long-term-care insurance, particularly if they begin to purchase it before age sixty-five, and the proportion able to do so should increase. These assumptions depend, however, on what we consider a "reasonable" contribution. Moreover, the willingness of people to make such expenditures is not clear.

Some studies looking at the feasibility of long-term-care insurance have assumed that the elderly could be expected to devote as much as 10 percent of their incomes to it. We know that many of the elderly already spend more than that for acute medical care, in out-of-pocket expenses and insurance premiums. The average of such liabilities was more than 11 percent for all the elderly in 1986.[24] If the costs of private long-term-care insurance averaged 6 to 8 percent of per capita incomes, the elderly would spend on the average up to 19 percent of their total incomes to meet health care needs. Those with fewer resources might spend 25 or 30 percent of their incomes. More probably, many elderly persons would view with skepticism the purchase of expensive insurance against the small possibility of a future catastrophe. Although the costs are lower for younger people, the risks also seem even more remote.

The findings of a six-state survey in 1982 of elderly purchasers of medigap insurance—a group with higher-than-average incomes and a demonstrated appreciation of the value of insurance—suggest that inducing purchase of long-term-care insurance may prove a formidable task.[25] First, more than a third of this group (37.9 percent) believed, erroneously, that Medicare and medigap insurance offered them protection against long-term-care needs.[26] Nearly half said they could not afford more than $20 a month; and fewer than 20 percent of the respondents could afford $50 a month. Yet in 1982 insurance costs for someone aged sixty-five would have run at least $40 and perhaps $60 a month. Affordability must, therefore, be a prime issue in marketing private long-term-care insurance.

Another important consideration is whether relatively expensive private insurance policies are a good buy. People with limited assets to protect might reasonably be expected to forgo buying insurance even if their incomes made it affordable. Assume, for example, that a couple will pay $1,000 a year for twenty years for such protection and will have a one-in-four chance of using it. Their assets would have to exceed $60,000 before they could expect to break even from this expenditure. A couple with $40,000 in assets could probably afford the insurance; it simply might not be an economically sound investment. It is this barrier as well as basic affordability that will deter many households with modest incomes from purchasing long-term-care insurance.

Policy Issues

Although this chapter focuses on the question whether future cohorts of the elderly can afford to protect themselves against long-term-care expenses, we have also implicitly raised issues that may require a public response. It may be necessary to foster private insurance in some way. But even after such insurance becomes more widely available, gaps in coverage and participation are likely. It is too soon to offer definitive answers. Rather, we suggest possible approaches and considerations as policy makers are increasingly called on to face the long-term-care problem.

The discussion about the ability of the elderly to finance their own long-term-care needs has roughly identified three groups, each with its own needs:

• elderly people with limited incomes and assets who are likely to rely on Medicaid for their long-term-care needs
• elderly or nearly elderly people who have sufficient resources to purchase private protection for long-term care either out of pocket or through private insurance
• elderly people who are not poor enough to become eligible for Medicaid readily but who cannot afford the costs of long-term-care insurance at retirement without making considerable sacrifices in their standard of living

Although some of tomorrow's elderly who will ultimately find themselves in the third group might be able to pay for long-term-care insurance today, they are not likely to do so under current market conditions. Moreover, this group also includes many people now over seventy, for whom purchase of long-term-care insurance is either not possible or not feasible because of the prohibitive cost.

Although we briefly consider policy options for each of these

153

groups, one of the most important issues is the extent to which policy trade-offs must be made that benefit one group at the expense of others. That is, if efforts are concentrated on subsidizing private long-term-care insurance for the second group—those already most able to fend for themselves—to what extent will that preclude extending protection to the third group? If Medicaid (or combined Medicaid-Medicare) benefits are extended to some members of the third group, will that discourage them from purchasing private insurance or saving for their potential long-term-care needs?

Improving Medicaid Coverage. Although we have not focused on the lowest-income elderly in this chapter, the issue of how far up the income distribution to extend Medicaid's protection is important. In theory all elderly people faced with enormous medical expenses that would wipe out their resources could receive Medicaid. Medicaid thus offers "last resort" protection. But for those with reasonable amounts of assets, Medicaid is essentially catastrophic protection available only after catastrophe strikes and they have spent down to eligibility levels. In contrast, private insurance would allow the elderly to preserve most of their assets in a financial emergency.

Consequently, one powerful and easily implemented improvement in Medicaid would be to limit how far people must spend down to become eligible for coverage. For example, couples might be allowed to divide their assets before spending down, so that the noninstitutionalized spouse could retain a reasonable amount of wealth. Such a policy would protect people who cannot afford to purchase insurance and might help reduce extralegal efforts to dispose of assets. It would also be a reasonable and limited expansion of government in the long-term-care area, if most of the burden is to be borne by private individuals and insurers. The proposed Medicare "catastrophic care" legislation includes a small-scale version of such a provision. Another area of needed expansion would be to include coverage for home care.

Encouraging Private Insurance. The main policy question facing the highest-income and the younger middle-income elderly is how to encourage the development and expansion of private insurance. The degree of public policy support might vary significantly, depending on assumptions about whether the private sector will respond effectively on its own.

First, and least expensive, would be to educate those facing retirement about what Medicare and medigap policies do and do not cover and what the need for and cost of long-term-care services are likely to be.[27] Presumably the combination of higher resources among the elderly and a greater understanding of the risks of long-term illness should stimulate demand for coverage.

Efforts to encourage the elderly to liquidate their assets—for example, through home equity conversion—might also be stressed, so that they could make more effective use of those assets. Home equity makes up a large proportion of the assets of the middle-income group; it is precisely those elderly persons who may believe they cannot afford premiums for insurance that total 5 percent or more of their incomes. Using a reverse annuity mortgage to prepay some or all of the costs of long-term-care insurance might increase the number of people able and willing to protect themselves. But what form should such efforts take, and to what extent should government become involved in fostering these markets?

Subsidies to employers or directly to workers nearing retirement might be used to encourage the purchase of long-term-care insurance. The traditional means of stimulating such activity is through the tax system. Is it reasonable, however, to subsidize those who can afford such insurance but are reluctant to purchase it? Such subsidies would be valuable to all families and individuals but would offer tax benefits mainly to those who would probably have purchased insurance anyway. Moreover, since those with the highest incomes have the most to protect, this subsidy might, like individual retirement accounts, primarily benefit the well-to-do. Even if tax credits, which offer equal dollar benefits regardless of one's tax bracket, were used, the benefits might be highly skewed. Only about 40 percent of the elderly have any tax liability; unless the credits were refundable, many people over sixty-five would not benefit from them.

These policy options for fostering reliance on private insurance concentrate on the demand side of the equation. But are insurers willing to offer such coverage? Again, tax inducements to insurers might be used. Alternatively, direct protection might be offered in the form of a government guarantee of benefits beyond a certain level of coverage. For example, if insurers offered a particular package of benefits, the government might pick up the costs for further care after a beneficiary had used more than a certain number of days of care. Capping the insurers' liability might encourage more inclusive benefits, covering, for example, mental disease and disorders, at a reasonable cost. But these tax advantages would still help mainly those motivated to buy insurance because they have assets they wish to protect.

The critical point in evaluating public expenditures directed mainly at high- and middle-income beneficiaries is whether they are likely to hold down other public costs. For example, one researcher has argued that private insurance coverage might reduce reliance on Medicaid by people who now spend down their assets, then rely on Medicaid to cover at least part of their health care costs.[28] But the federal and state savings achieved might or might not be as great as the costs of some of the policy options to stimulate coverage. Moreover, they might do the most good for those least in need—those most able to cover long-term-care expenses on their own.

Helping Those Caught in the Middle. A large number of the lower-middle-income elderly are likely to fall through the cracks in a combined private insurance–Medicaid approach to financing long-term care. Moreover, since private coverage is not a feasible option for most people now over seventy, many of the older elderly will remain relatively unprotected for some time. Some of the policy options discussed could shrink the group adversely affected, by expanding Medicaid or making private coverage more affordable. Nonetheless, gaps will remain.

A more efficient, piecemeal option would be to offer a public program aimed at the group now caught in the middle. The primary advantage of such an approach would rest in minimizing government costs and involvement. But it also raises the problem of coordination with Medicaid and private insurance. A targeted public-sector program—perhaps sponsored by state governments—might allow people to buy insurance that exempted a certain amount of assets from Medicaid spend-down rules and offered improved protection against impoverishment of the husband or wife left in the community. The spend-down requirement might be eased considerably for persons who buy the insurance—perhaps to $25,000 or $30,000 plus the home.

Such a program might also establish income-related premiums. This kind of program would obviously be aimed at the modest-income family. Those with substantial assets would find it advantageous to seek other means of protecting them, for example, by purchasing private insurance. This strategy implicitly assumes that higher-income families would not need tax advantages or other stimuli to encourage them to purchase private coverage.

A second possibility would be an income-related premium under Medicare—probably administered through the income tax system. The elderly who did not have private long-term-care insurance would be covered by Medicare or a separate long-term-care program, effective above some deductible. Medicaid's main role under such a system might be to pay the deductible for lower-income persons. Medicare beneficiaries would pay a premium of some fixed proportion of their incomes. At the same time the payroll tax might be raised slightly to help keep the program affordable and maintain the insurance principle of spreading costs over a longer period. Nonetheless, the bulk of the financing burden would fall on persons sixty-five and over. Purchasers of private insurance might be allowed to waive this long-term-care eligibility and claim a tax credit up to some percentage of the Medicare surcharge. Such provisions could help maintain a private insurance effort.

Finally, another option might be to deemphasize the emerging private long-term-care insurance market and, instead, to provide some well-controlled amount of long-term-care services in return for a new, income-related insurance premium aimed at everyone. The premium might be phased in gradually on an age-adjusted basis—perhaps beginning at forty, for example. This would keep costs low for all citizens. Furthermore, because the premium would be tied to the income tax structure, it would be less burdensome for people with modest incomes. To control costs and use, the premium might be combined with a relatively large annual deductible, perhaps with a lifetime limit.

Current lack of political support for such expanded government coverage may preclude this option, and other problems would arise even if it were pursued. One of the more difficult issues would be to establish when the new coverage would begin. If today's elderly were "grandfathered" into the system, the initial costs would be high. Moreover, such a policy might add fuel to the current debate over intergenerational equity and the extent to which the elderly of this generation are beneficiaries of windfall gains that will not be available in the future. Moreover, it might be tempting to use the Old Age, Survivors, Disability, and Health Insurance (OASDHI) trust fund reserves to fund long-term care for the current generation. If so, instead of asking today's elderly—and tomorrow's good times generation—to help pay for their own long-term care, we would be benefiting them at the expense of the retirement funds of their children.

One possible approach to mitigating the start-up costs while offering relief to those in need would be to establish a higher initial deductible that could be reduced over time. In this way individuals would implicitly receive credit for the years they contributed to the insurance plan. Medicaid's role might largely become one of paying the deductible for this broader long-term-care insurance.

Conclusions

We began this chapter by asking whether the elderly can afford long-term care. The implicit answer to that question is that they already do. With Medicaid as a last resort, individuals and their families now directly bear the costs of such care. These costs are devastating for a few and raise the fear of such devastation for many more. The more interesting and challenging question is whether there are better ways to provide for the costs of long-term care.

We conclude that, for some of the elderly, Medicaid's role is critical and should be expanded to provide a better floor of protection. For perhaps as many as half of Americans aged fifty to seventy, however, private insurance could play an important role. Yet the potential of private insurance is just starting to be realized, and many who could afford it are not likely to be willing to purchase it. Some public support may be needed to stimulate the market for such insurance and to increase public awareness of both the costs and the benefits.

Most troublesome are the elderly with lower (but above poverty-level) incomes or of advanced age who are unlikely to be well served by private insurance. Currently their major option is to experience catastrophic losses and then rely on Medicaid. But the resultant losses may be devastating to the pride and independence of people who survive the episode of long-term care or to their spouses, who may be left behind with severely limited resources. Moreover, from a government cost perspective, this situation may prove penny-wise and pound-foolish. If a limited extension of government protection could prevent this group's dependence on Medicaid and on other means-tested government programs such as Supplemental Security Income for the surviving spouse, the results might be less costly in the long run for all concerned. Alternatively, the problems of patching together three long-term-care "systems" may necessitate a much expanded role for the federal government—at least in providing the means of coordinating and financing a coherent long-term policy.

Notes

1. C. Ross, S. Danziger, and E. Smolensky, "Social Security, Work Effort, and Poverty among Elderly Men, 1939–1979," Institute for Research on Poverty Discussion Paper 785–85 (Madison: University of Wisconsin, 1985); and E. Wolff, "Estimates of Household Wealth Inequality in the U.S., 1962–1983" (Paper presented to the Nineteenth General Conference of the IARIW, Nourdwis-Kerhout, Netherlands, July 1985).

2. R. Avery, G. Elliehausen, G. Canner, and T. Gustafson, "Survey of Consumer Finances, 1983," *Federal Reserve Bulletin* (September 1984), pp. 679–92.

3. M. Moon and I. Sawhill, "Changes in Income Distribution," in J. Palmer and I. Sawhill, eds., *The Reagan Record* (Cambridge, Mass.: Ballinger, 1984).

4. S. Grad, *Income of the Population 55 and Over, 1980,* Social Security Administration publication no. 13-11871 (Washington, D.C., 1984); and B. Torrey, "Sharing Increasing Costs on Declining Income: The Visible Dilemma of the Invisible Aged," *MMFO/Health and Society,* vol. 63, no. 2 (1986), pp. 377–94.

5. N. Gordon, "Statements on the Elderly and Health Care Expenditures" before Subcommittee on Health and the Environment, Committee on Energy and Commerce, U.S. House of Representatives (Washington, D.C.: U.S. Congressional Budget Office, 1986), mimeo; J. Quinn, "The Economic Status of the Elderly: Beware of the Mean," *Review of Income and Wealth* (1986); T. Smeeding, "Nonmoney Income and the Elderly: The Case of the 'Tweener,' " *Journal of Policy Analysis and Management* (1986); T. Smeeding and L. Straub, "Health Care Finance among the Elderly: Who Really Pays the Bills?" *Journal of Health Politics, Policy, and Law* (1986); and B. Soldo and C. Longino, "Social and Physical Environments for the Vulnerable Aged" (Paper prepared for the Symposium on a Social Environment for an Aging Society, National Research Council, Washington, D.C., December 8–11, 1985).

6. Gordon, "Statements on the Elderly."

7. The "reference person" is the same as the householder or the person considered the head of the household. In this chapter an elderly unit, elderly family, or elderly household is considered to be a unit (family, household) with a reference person (household head) age sixty-five or older.

8. Wolff, "Estimates of Household Wealth Inequality."

9. D. Radner and D. Vaughn, "The Joint Distribution of Wealth and Income for Age Groups, 1979," in E. Wolff, ed., *International Comparisons of the Distribution of Household Wealth* (New York: New York University, 1986).

10. Of the 27.9 percent of elderly units with incomes above $12,848, less than 4 percent had net worths below $20,120 in 1979. While these persons may be in some danger of losing their savings if they should need nursing home care, it is unlikely—given their incomes and assets—that they would lose all their assets (and spend down to Medicaid eligibility levels) unless, for instance, both spouses required nursing home stays for above-average lengths of time.

11. A bill of $17,000 in 1979 would be comparable to the $23,000 figure mentioned earlier.

12. The Medicare Catastrophic Act of 1988 (P.L. 100-360) now offers protection against impoverishment to the at-home spouses of nursing home residents. States must permit these spouses to keep at least $786 a month in income (up to a maximum of $1,500) and $12,000 in assets (up to a maximum of $60,000) without losing Medicaid benefits for their institutionalized spouse.

13. P. Doty, K. Liu, and J. Weiner, "An Overview of Long Term Care," *Health Care Financing Review* (Spring 1985), pp.69–78.

14. J. Poterba and L. Summers, "Public Policy Implications of Declining Old-Age Mortality" (Paper presented to the Brookings Conference on Retirement and Aging, May 2, 1985).

15. Doty et al., "An Overview."

16. R. Arnett, C. Cowell, L. Davidoff, and M. Freeland, "Health Spending

Trends in the 1980s: Adjusting to Financial Incentives," *Health Care Financing Review*, vol. 6, no. 3 (Spring 1985), pp. 1–26.

17. Public Health Service, *The National Nursing Home Survey: 1977 Summary for the United States* (Washington, D.C., 1979).

18. Government Accounting Office, "Medicaid and Nursing Home Care: Cost Increases and the Need for Services Are Creating Problems for the State and the Elderly" (Washington, D.C., 1983).

19. Medicare has historically been the largest payer for *medical* home health services. Cost estimates for custodial services are much more difficult to obtain.

20. For a more thorough analysis of private long-term-care insurance, see the chapter by Lewin and Wallack in this volume. Our discussion of long-term-care insurance is primarily aimed at reaching a reasonable estimate of costs that can be compared with ability to pay.

21. M. Meiners, "The State of the Art in Long-Term Care Insurance," National Center for Health Services Research, 1984.

22. M. Meiners, "The Case for Long Term Care Insurance," *Health Affairs*, vol. 2 (Summer 1983), pp. 55–79.

23. U.S. Bureau of the Census, *Money Income and Poverty Status of Families and Persons in the U.S.: 1984*, Series P-6, no. 189 (Washington, D.C., 1985).

24. J. Feder, M. Moon, and W. Scanlon, "Medicare Reform: Nibbling at Catastrophic Costs," *Health Affairs*, vol. 6, no. 4 (Winter 1987), pp. 5–19.

25. M. Meiners and A. Tave, "Consumer Interest in Long Term Care Insurance: A Survey of the Elderly in Six States," National Center for Health Services Research, 1985, mimeo.

26. A survey for the AARP found that nearly 80 percent of the elderly thought they were already covered for long-term care.

27. An education campaign to indicate what *private* long-term-care insurance does and does not cover may also be in order.

28. Meiners, "The Case for Long Term Care Insurance."

10
Strategies for Financing Long-Term Care

Marion Ein Lewin and Stanley Wallack

How to provide for the long-term care of tomorrow's elderly citizens is today an issue receiving widespread attention. Concerns about the inexorable aging of our population, with its implications for added public expenditures to meet growing chronic care needs, are being raised at a time of changing public policy and unrelenting pressures for federal deficit reduction. States as well find themselves financially strapped as they contend with escalating Medicaid budgets and competing demands for limited resources. In this context, the improved economic status of the aging cohort is encouraging the consideration of private sector financing options. These options are aimed at more broadly and affordably redistributing the burden of financing long-term care to prevent the indignity of impoverishment and to reduce dependence on Medicaid. Increasing interest is therefore being focused on the potential for risk-pooling mechanisms that might fill some of the large gaps in present health care coverage.

Recent expansion of Medicare to cover the catastrophic costs associated primarily with acute illness has brought into even sharper relief the inadequacy of our long-term-care financing. Nursing home payments are the largest single out-of-pocket health care expense of the elderly. According to the National Center for Health Services Research (NCHSR), 80 percent of the aged who spend more than $2,000 out-of-pocket do so not for acute care but for long-term care.

In the past few years a market for private long-term-care insurance has begun to emerge. So far the market has been small, with the coverage offered limited primarily to indemnity payments for nursing home care. Until now only a narrow sector of the elderly population has been attracted to and purchased a long-term-care benefit. But today, coverage options are changing and expanding rapidly.

Private insurance for long-term care has had only a limited market test. Yet many have already concluded that these private sector risk-pooling options hold small potential for ameliorating this country's impending long-term-care funding crisis.

Others argue that, although private long-term-care insurance could substitute for the out-of-pocket expenses some of the elderly incur, it may only minimally reduce Medicaid spending. Estimates of potential public sector savings, however, have been based on the two- to three-year nursing home benefit limitations characteristic of early long-term-care insurance products. Policies and plans now being developed provide lengthier if not unlimited coverage and hold the promise of greater savings for the Medicaid program.

Clearly, there are no panaceas in this area; private sector strategies can be only part of the solution. The verdict on their potential to meet the funding challenges ahead, however, should not be based on the limited track record of first-generation products.

These options stand a much better chance of being successful and affordable as:

- Americans become more aware of the need for improved long-term-care protection
- better data become available to help insurers and health care organizations gain more understanding of the elderly market
- risk-sharing models are developed that more effectively blend the objectives and capabilities of the public and private sectors

Given the improbability of major expansion of public financing in this arena, private financing efforts need to be more fully and fairly explored.

The Challenges of a Graying America

The pressure to do something about long-term care is growing as the demographic explosion continues on a collision course with constrained public funding. By the year 2000, an estimated 32 million Americans will be aged sixty-five and over. This group will constitute about 20 percent of the population by 2015. Furthermore, the older elderly, who are more apt to be frail, constitute the fastest-growing segment: the number of Americans aged eighty-five and over is now twenty-two times as large as in 1900.

With the "graying" of America, the nation's nursing home bill is rising. Annual expenditures climbed from $27.2 billion in 1982 to $38 billion in 1986 and are expected to grow to $129 billion in 2000.[1]

Medicaid has become the principal source of public financing for nursing home care, paying for 42 percent of total costs. Medicare and private insurance pay less than 3 percent, while the remaining costs of long-term care are almost all paid out-of-pocket by individuals and families.[2]

Americans save relatively little of their income, less than citizens of many societies that provide universal government-funded long-term care. For many elderly, access to public financing is associated with "spending down" to Medicaid eligibility for long-term-care needs.

According to a study in Massachusetts by the Harvard Medical School and the state's Blue Cross and Blue Shield plans, approximately 46 percent of persons seventy-five and over who live alone would spend down to impoverishment after only thirteen weeks in a nursing home. After two years in a nursing home, between 80 percent and 90 percent of elderly people would be pauperized.[3] The Health Care Financing Administration (HCFA) estimates that almost half the patients Medicaid pays for in nursing homes are not eligible on entry but spend down their resources and become eligible.[4]

The feasibility and desirability of risk-sharing arrangements for long-term care, both to provide financial protection and to preserve scarce public funding for those aged unable to finance their own long-term care, are widely debated. The dimensions of the long-term-care problem for the elderly are similar to those of other problems that have been dealt with effectively by risk pooling. The lifetime risk of someone over sixty-five entering a nursing home is between 20 percent and 45 percent.[5] If people saved for the possibility of nursing home care, about 65 percent would oversave and forgo spending that would benefit them or their children.

Some have pointed to the merits, if not the necessity, of a major federal role in this area, one that would enable risk pooling across the broadest possible base. The federal tax system through either the IRS or through payroll taxation would be a likely vehicle. As our national checkbook goes deeper into the red, however, the near-term likelihood of moving in this direction appears remote.

Others contend that the chief responsibility for long-term care should reside in the states, as they can carry out the necessary coordination of services and management tasks better than the federal government. An issue of concern here is the growing difference in economic conditions across states, markedly influencing their tax capacities, revenues, and budgets. Moreover, the elderly are not evenly distributed across the country; almost half live in eight states (California, Florida, Illinois, Michigan, New York, Ohio, Pennsylvania, and Texas). Many of the states with the largest elderly populations will lack the resources to meet their needs.

Against this background, the challenge of fashioning effective public and private partnerships to promote the development of private long-term-care insurance is receiving heightened attention. More careful scrutiny of such options is also being spurred by the increased affluence of the elderly. According to the Congressional Budget Office, "After accounting for inflation, the average cash income of families with elderly members increased by nearly 18 percent during the 15-year period from 1969 to 1984, the latest year for which detailed data are available—while the average income of unrelated elderly individuals rose by 34 percent."[6] Per capita income for today's elderly is roughly equivalent to that for the nonelderly population as the incidence of poverty has declined from 25 percent in 1970 to less than 13 percent, lower than the rate for all U.S. citizens. Furthermore, nearly 75 percent of this group own homes, and about 83 percent have paid off their mortgages.[7]

Private and public employee pensions supply a growing source of income for the elderly. In 1984, 34 percent of older Americans received income from a private pension. Among higher-income elderly (those with family income at twice the poverty level or more) 43 percent reported pension income.[8] Moreover, the future elderly are more likely than today's new retirees to have employer-provided pensions at retirement. This trend can be explained in part by the longer tenure of young workers in a post-ERISA work force, compared with workers now retiring. Projections indicate that between the 1980s and the year 2020, the real disposable income of the elderly will continue to grow significantly.[9]

Despite the rising prosperity of the elderly, however, large variations in income among this population remain. In 1987, 7.4 million of the nation's 27 million elderly Americans were poor or near-poor.[10] And almost half the elderly report incomes within 200 percent of the poverty level. A disproportionate number of elderly poor or near-poor over age seventy-five are single women—the cohort most vulnerable to costly institutionalization.

Developing a Private Market in Long-Term Care: Initial Efforts

Private risk-pooling options specifically targeted to financing long-term care are relatively new phenomena, and activity in this arena has focused primarily on development of long-term-care insurance products. A 1988 survey conducted by the Health Insurance Association indicated that thirty of its member companies are selling long-term-care policies of some type. A compilation by a Department of Health and Human Services Task Force on Long-Term Care Policies reported that seventy companies are now selling this type of coverage and that more than 400,000 elderly have purchased long-term-care policies.[11]

Reflecting insurers' uncertainty and anxieties about the long-term-care market, most of the plans sold have been individual, unindexed indemnity plans, paying a fixed amount per day for covered illnesses. The plans offer different lengths of coverage and contain waiting-period provisions designed to help limit inappropriate use of benefits. Other controls frequently applied include medical screens, physician reviews, prior hospitalization, restrictions on coverage of preexisting conditions, exclusion of mental and nervous disorders, and renewability limitations. For most plans, premiums are determined by age and time of purchase and vary depending on the coverage desired. They can vary from $700 per year for a person age sixty-five to $1,500 a year or more for persons age seventy-nine.[12]

First-generation, free-standing long-term-care insurance has represented a small and selective market. Large carriers have remained skittish about entering what they view as an experimental and risky line of coverage. Some of the perceived barriers to successful marketing of such plans have been well noted. Among them is a concern over adverse selection (the likelihood that people most at risk of needing long-term care will purchase coverage, while others will not) and the problem of "moral hazard" (the increased demand and use stimulated by insurance). Controlling the use of benefits is viewed as a particularly vexing issue, since currently 75 percent of the disabled elderly who live in the community rely solely on unpaid informal care.[13] For every nursing home resident, it is estimated that two or three equally impaired persons remain in the community.[14] Using Paringer's estimated ratio of the value of family effort to expenditures for nursing home care, the commercial value of informal long-term care in 1985 was $22 billion—approximately 90 percent of that related to care for the elderly.[15]

The difficulty of developing an insurance product without adequate experience from which to make actuarial calculations represents another concern. Pricing a benefit that may not be paid out until far in the future is also problematic. Further, serious questions are posed about the insurability of custodial services, which account for a large portion of extended-care needs, and the other social support services beyond the current scope of insurance coverage.

Regulatory issues also form barriers to market growth. Since insurance is overseen by states, insurers currently face an array of conflicting regulations in different parts of the country. Because long-term-care insurance integrates concepts of life and health insurance, questions relating to the proportion of premiums either paid out or reserved annually in benefits and to the tax treatment of premiums, investment income, and reserves need to be reassessed. Many of the technical and consumer issues may be resolved by careful policy design and by creating a regulatory environment more conducive to nurturing long-term-care products. In the past few years, many high-level public and private sector task forces have been convened to make specific recommendations that would address the stumbling blocks to broader market development

Barriers to and Opportunities for Market Growth

A number of other factors, however, are often considered more fundamental impediments to product growth in this area. They relate to perceptions of coverage, the "spend-down" features of the Medicaid program, "affordability," and the key issue of marketing.

Perception of Coverage. Until recently the majority of the elderly population perceived themselves as adequately covered for long-term-care expenses through Medicare and supplemental insurance (medigap). Several years ago a survey by the American Association of Retired Persons (AARP) found that 79 percent of the elderly believed that Medicare covered most of the costs of nursing home care; 50 percent of all respondents believed supplemental insurance would pay all or part. If there is one point of agreement, it is that the demand for private insurance will be enhanced if people become more aware of the risks and costs associated with the need for long-term care and the limitations of existing coverage.

Changing demographics and growing documentation by public forums and the media on the inadequacy of current long-term-care protection are rapidly producing a more informed and sophisticated consumer. In contrast to the earlier AARP survey, for example, a more recent poll indicated that more than 60 percent of the American public have experienced—in their own families or through close friends—the need for long-term care.[16]

Insurers believe that adult children will become increasingly interested in purchasing private insurance for their elderly parents. Being part of a three- or four-generation family—children in their fifties and sixties responsible for parents in their eighties and nineties—is becoming a regular, rather than a rare, phenomenon. Children are increasingly experiencing firsthand the burden, both financial and otherwise, of having to take care of a chronically ill parent. Based on industry estimates, 20 percent of the work force are now faced with having to care for an elderly relative, and that proportion is expected to grow.[17] The need for protection against the catastrophic costs that can result comes closer to home every day.

The Medicaid "Safety Net." Together with misconceptions about the extent of coverage, insurers believe that the Medicaid "safety net" also contributes to the environment unfavorable for the development of long-term-care insurance. At one of the first national conferences to investigate private options for financing long-term care, sponsored by HCFA, a well-known industry official suggested that "the major potential competitor in long-term care is not other insurers, not other financial service institutions, nor private savings, but the government: generally, the Medicaid program is perceived by the middle class as free, acceptable, and an inalienable right."[18] Other studies suggest, however, that the welfare stigma of Medicaid, its institutional bias, and uncertainties about who can expect to receive benefits make the program less an impediment to market growth than often perceived.

Although it cannot be proved, many middle-class elderly, faced with catastrophic long-term-care expenditures, may transfer their assets to family members or to a trust specifically to become eligible for Medicaid nursing home benefits. Some analysts estimate that Medicaid could recover more than $500 million over current collections if states stepped up their estate recovery programs.[19]

The vexing dilemma of nonpoor elderly divesting or spending down their assets to become eligible for Medicaid has been caused largely by the Catch-22 nature of current long-term-care financing. To obtain any public funding for catastrophic chronic care, patient, spouse, or family must exhaust all their resources down to the welfare eligibility level. Many states are actively investigating risk-pooling arrangements to enable middle-class elderly to protect themselves against unpredictable and costly long-term-care outlays, while maintaining their independence and avoiding impoverishment.

Affordability. Affordability of premiums appears to be a key requirement for the successful development of a private long-term-care insurance market. The market potential for long-term-care policies is seen to rest primarily with the more affluent elderly: individuals with incomes of at least $10,000 and couples with incomes in the $15,000 range.[20] More specific projections about the size of the market vary widely, however, depending on assumptions made about affordability, the extent of discretionary income, and the estimated cost of insurance coverage. Perhaps most important, capacity to afford private long-term-care insurance may have little relation to the preference and willingness of those who could pay for such coverage actually to purchase it.

Over the years numerous studies have tried to measure the potential market for long-term-care insurance. A study conducted at Brandeis University's Bigel Institute looked at older persons with incomes between $10,000 and $15,000 per year and concluded that, after paying for food, housing, medical expenses, clothing, and transportation, 35 percent of their income remained for discretionary expenditures. These data show that the purchase of a long-term-care benefit is a viable option for a considerable segment of the elderly population.[21]

Premium costs and affordability have been found to be most sensitive to age at the time of purchase. If, for example, one-fifth of the elderly over eighty-five are in a nursing home, spreading the cost of nursing home care, about $30,000 annually, among all eighty-five-year-olds will still present financial hardships for many, since it would entail an annual payment of $6,000 (20 percent of $30,000), or $500 a month for each person. If we spread the cost across all people sixty-five and older (about 5 percent are in nursing homes), the cost would be about $1,500 a year (5 percent of $30,000). Obviously, prefunding or subsidization across age groups needs to occur if the majority of our elderly are to be financially protected.

A significant portion of the current long-term-care insurance premium is associated with marketing expenses—primarily the costs of individual selling and underwriting—as well as with the risks inherent in individual lines of insurance. Through mechanisms like group marketing and reinsurance, long-term-care coverage could be put within the reach of larger numbers of the elderly. Such coverage could stabilize, if not reduce, Medicaid outlays.

Substantial benefits could ensue if only middle-income elderly participated in an insurance plan. Using an example of one hundred median-income sixty-five-year-olds, Brandeis University researchers have estimated that under current financing options Medicaid might end up paying one-third of this cohort's total long-term-care costs. If, however, these people purchased a long-term-care policy with a lifetime nursing home benefit, a policy comparable to that already being offered by a number of continuing care communities, then Medicaid costs would fall to zero. This, in fact, has been the experience in life-care communities that offer a full-guarantee policy; that is, nursing home coverage at no or little additional cost above monthly fees.

Marketing. How to strengthen and enhance the demand for private long-term-care insurance remains a timely issue, raising many unanswered questions. Some of the major impediments to market growth—misperceptions about coverage, the need to move away from individual fixed-indemnity plans to prefunded group policies that are adjusted for inflation, and the importance of getting individuals to purchase policies at a younger age—have already been discussed. Acquiring data for insurers to design more comprehensive benefits, to assess risks fully, or to price products with certainty remains a serious concern. But sales and market experience and new research and survey findings are producing a rapid, if still incomplete, body of information. Better data on the lifetime risk and cost of nursing home use among the elderly indicate that such costs are distributed unequally—only 13 percent of the elderly account for 90 percent of all nursing home expenditures. These data support the desirability and feasibility of long-term-care risk-sharing arrangements.[22] A number of other issues, however, also deserve attention, since they may be key factors in galvanizing broader support for long-term-care products.

How to build a more robust market for long-term-care risk-sharing options and how to overcome problems related to adverse selection are two of the more formidable challenges to developing a more successful product. Experience with first-generation products, however, is providing some valuable insights. As insurers assess demand and need carefully, it is becoming clear that potential purchasers are interested in this type of protection for a variety of reasons. These include protecting assets, ensuring access to quality care, preserving some independence, and preventing impoverishment.

Because expenditures related to nursing home care represent the most visible and largest component of long-term-care costs, conventional products have focused primarily on coverage for institutional care, providing some asset protection. But since most existing indemnity products are unindexed for inflation, their value declines over time.

Numerous surveys have shown, however, that the elderly appear more interested in risk-sharing plans that provide options and support for staying in their own home than in stand-alone nursing home indemnity coverage. A frequent criticism of free-standing long-term-care insurance is that it perpetuates a system biased toward acute care and institutional care. Such a system is not appropriate, desirable, or cost effective in addressing the spectrum of long-term-care needs. Underwriting long-term care, a benefit fraught with concerns about moral hazard and adverse selection, essentially requires effective risk management if such coverage is to be adequate, marketable, and affordable.

Responding to Market Demand—Second Generation Products

Market experience underscores the elderly's strong preference for home health care and independent living over a stand-alone nursing home benefit. Insurers are responding by liberalizing their home health care coverage, using case management to encourage more prudent use of costly medical services. Today considerable attention focuses on models that integrate financing and delivery, such as traditional health maintenance organizations (HMOs), social/health maintenance organizations (S/HMOs), and continuing care retirement communities (CCRCs).

Insurers, jointly venturing with HMOs, have begun to experiment with offering enrollees wraparound coverage in the form of a comprehensive long-term-care benefit. A leading demonstration in this area involves the Group Health Cooperative of Puget Sound, a staff model HMO with 350,000 members, approximately 10 percent of whom are over age sixty-five. The HMO has undertaken a venture with the Metropolitan Life Insurance Company of New York that is being watched with interest for several reasons. First, it offers the potential of building a more viable risk pool composed of younger elderly people. Second, it represents the marriage of two kinds of expertise considered fundamental to the effective development of affordable long-term-care coverage. These are an HMO's ability to lower the threshold price of health care coverage by managing utilization and an insurer's ability to price and underwrite a benefit on the basis of actuarially sound calculations of entrance, frequency, and duration.

The HCFA-sponsored S/HMO demonstration program is an effort to apply many of the proven concepts of HMOs to long-term care. Under this Medicare demonstration, almost 10,000 elderly persons are enrolled in four S/HMOs across the country. Using case management, S/HMOs have been able to offer the elderly a broader, more coordinated set of benefits financed through savings on the acute care side that can be used to help pay for expanded long-term services. The S/HMO demonstration suggests that an extensive home health care benefit can be provided within a prescribed budget through a managed insurance plan.

For some middle-class elderly, evidence is gathering that financial protection alone or even the promise of more comprehensive benefits may not be compelling reasons to purchase long-term-care coverage. This is especially true for the large number of elderly who do not believe that they are in imminent need of long-term care. Many of these elderly are more interested in protecting a desired life style that will ensure access to high-quality services without disrupting family relationships or their living environment. Continuing care retirement communities are responding to this market demand. These communities extend protection beyond simply the catastrophic costs of long-term care to include the promise of high-quality housing, a secure environment, and a well-managed delivery system that ensures the elderly access to complete health care and chronic care services, without the threat of impoverishment.

Since these communities typically require a large up-front payment of $60,000 to $100,000 and monthly fees of $1,000 or more, this option is available primarily to the wealthy aged. Studies indicate that perhaps 10 percent of the elderly could afford to join a continuing care community. Researchers at the Wharton Business School at the University of Pennsylvania and at Brandeis University, suggest that many middle-income elderly could afford CCRCs.[23] With support from the Robert Wood Johnson Foundation, efforts are now under way at Brandeis University to assess the marketability of a less costly "off-campus" model CCRC: a life-care-at-home plan without a housing component. The Robert Wood Johnson Foundation and the Pew Charitable Trusts are also jointly testing market interest in an at-home life care program for middle-income elderly in northeast Philadelphia.

These days, the market for long-term-care insurance appears to be actively growing. New and improved products, with options likely to be more attractive and affordable to a larger segment of the population, are becoming available or are in the design stage. A number of developments are adding impetus to these efforts.

Advocates of private risk pooling are convinced that the ultimate effectiveness of these options rests on the success of marketing group coverage, as opposed to individual indemnity. Clearly, group products broaden the risk pool to include younger, healthier populations that can subsidize the current cost of older participants. Further, groups offer better vehicles to educate individuals about the risks of long-term care and the need for adequate protection. Through group products, lower premiums can be achieved and the risk of adverse selection reduced.

While until recently virtually all nursing home policies have been sold to individuals, a number of large insurance companies such as Aetna Life and Casualty, the Travelers Companies, and John Hancock Financial Services have begun to sell their products to employer groups. The Travelers Corporation in Hartford, Connecticut, was the first to move long-term care into the employee benefit market, using case management principles and group experience to limit expenses. Travelers offers nursing home, home health, and adult day coverage to its existing groups of 10,000 or more. Rates are age related, with provisions for portability and the opportunity to insure other immediate family members (including parents). Employers will pay premiums through payroll deductions. Two major noninsurance companies—Procter & Gamble Co. and American Express—have also begun to offer carrier-provided long-term-care coverage to their workers as an employee benefit.

In other market developments, the AARP has signed over 15,000 members for its long-term-care insurance program. This is a second-generation product with expanded home health care benefits and without the three-day prior hospitalization requirement that characterized almost all first-generation products. AARP is now developing a managed-care product that further integrates home- and community-based services. Harvard Community Health Plan, a large non-profit HMO, provides yet another example of a new and innovative initiative. It plans to enter the continuing care retirement business and extend the HMO approach to life care.

Current pressures on companies to hold down health care expenditures and to limit expansion of unfunded liability for retiree health benefits have accelerated interest in the possibility of using individual retirement accounts, pensions, or life insurance benefits to pay for long-term-care insurance. As a result of a state-administration-initiated plan, Alaska, together with Aetna, has started offering long-term-care insurance to 7,500 retired state workers and their spouses. Under the program, beneficiaries will pay their health-related premiums from their pension checks. Similarly, the U.S. Office of Personnel Management, which administers the Federal Employee Health Benefits Program, is considering a plan to offer federal employees the opportunity to convert part of their life insurance benefit to cover part of the premium cost of a long-term-care plan.

Both state and federal tax incentives to encourage the purchase of employment-based group plans could be a major stimulant to market growth. Unlike health insurance, employer contributions to long-term-care insurance are not fully deductible. If contracts are funded with level premiums, which they usually are, current laws do not provide for full deductions by either employers or employees. States that are particularly interested in broadening private long-term-care coverage in light of their mounting Medicaid nursing home expenditures are seriously considering creating a more favorable tax environment for such products. Over twenty states have initiatives under way to develop a market for long-term-care insurance and to protect the elderly consumers from inadequate products.[24] Under the Robert Wood Johnson Foundation's program to promote long-term-care insurance for the elderly, six states have received grants to foster effective public-private partnerships in which insurers are encouraged to develop quality products while spreading the risk of long-term costs.

Despite these encouraging activities, the perception remains that the private sector will not enter this market more aggressively until it believes it can better define and control its risks. To guard against large and unpredictable losses when medical necessity is not the basis for service coverage and to keep premiums reasonably affordable, most private plans have limited nursing home coverage to three years. To encourage broader interest in the purchase of private long-term-care policies, the notion of having Medicaid or Medicare share in the risk of truly catastrophic long-term-care outlays through reinsurance or stop-loss mechanisms is receiving increased attention. In the majority of cases, Medicaid already pays for these extended nursing home stays. Many states, therefore, are looking into expanding private financing of short-term protection by guaranteeing Medicaid coverage, without the spend-down requirement, for those elderly who have exhausted their benefits. Indiana has already passed such legislation. On the federal level Senator George J. Mitchell (Democrat-Maine) has introduced a measure that would provide Medicare coverage for nursing home and other long-term care services after a two-year deductible period had elapsed. During the two-year period the deductible would be paid with private funds, insurance, or Medicaid. Reinsurance might also be made more widely available through the private sector alone, financed by a small add-on to premiums. As these kinds of strategies are further explored, the potential cost of publicly financed reinsurance must be weighed against the hoped-for benefits—more comprehensive and varied coverage options, more affordably priced.

Conclusion

How to meet the chronic and long-term-care needs of tomorrow's elderly has become a critical public policy concern. The national debate over enhancing Medicare coverage for the catastrophic costs associated with acute care has focused attention on this largest gap in current health care coverage. While government, in some respects, may be the most appropriate vehicle for providing a long-term-care benefit, fiscal realities make such an option less than likely.

The capability for private financing of long-term care is higher than once thought, and, in varying degrees, these programs are potentially affordable to many of the elderly. The improved economic status of the aging cohort has heightened interest in the potential of private sector financing alternatives that could more broadly and affordably redistribute the burden of financing long-term care to protect the assets of the elderly, prevent the indignity of impoverishment, and reduce dependence on Medicaid.

Until only recently, the market for long-term-care insurance has been small and specialized, focused primarily on offering a limited nursing home indemnity benefit. Today, products have begun to respond more effectively to market demand and to the awareness that the elderly have different perceptions about risk and the kind of arrangements they want to make to protect themselves against it. Many of the newer approaches and options seek to integrate acute and long-term-care services in a managed-care setting. Group plans as well as life care products that combine health, housing, and continuing care have begun to be marketed. These increasingly viable private sector options can perhaps address the long-term-care requirements of much of our elderly population or of their adult children concerned about the welfare of parents reaching old age. The success of these kinds of efforts may help us to reshape existing public programs to serve more effectively those elderly Americans in greatest need. Our financing strategy for solving the catastrophic cost of long-term care cannot disregard the objectives or desires of the elderly. They want help in maintaining their independence and life style and not just in paying for their long-term stays in a nursing home.

Although significant product development is taking place, the importance of educating the elderly about the need for long-term-care protection and generating additional data to define this market and its risks better demands further attention. Providing tax incentives to make long-term care part of the employee benefit package or to enhance the attractiveness of converting some portion of an individual's pension or life insurance plan into a long-term-care benefit could greatly bolster market growth in this area. Forging creative private-public partnerships to help us achieve some of these goals is our best hope for meeting the formidable challenge of humanely and effectively providing for the long-term-care needs of an aging population in an era of limited resources.

174

Notes

1. See Health Care Financing Administration, "National Health Expenditures, 1986–2000," *Health Care Financing Review* (Summer 1987), pp. 1–35.
2. Nancy M. Gordon, *Hearings on the Economic Status of the Elderly*, U.S. Congress, House, Subcommittee on Health and the Environment, Committee on Energy and Commerce, 100th Congress, 1st session, March 26, 1986, pp. 13–14.
3. U.S. House of Representatives Select Committee on Aging, "America's Elderly at Risk" (Washington, D.C., 1985), p. 19.
4. See Marian Gornick et al., "Twenty Years of Medicare and Medicaid: Covered Populations, Use of Benefits, and Program Expenditures," *Health Care Financing Review* (1985 Annual Supplement), pp. 13–59.
5. Department of Health and Human Services Task Force on Long-Term Health Care Policies, "Fact Sheet on Long-Term Care," April 8, 1987, p. 2.
6. Gordon, *Economic Status of the Elderly*, p. 2.
7. Task Force on Long-Term Health Care Policies, p. 2.
8. ICF, Incorporated, "Prevention and Elimination of Poverty among the Elderly Living Alone" (Paper presented to the Commonwealth Fund Commission on Elderly People Living Alone, New York, May 1986).
9. Ibid.
10. Diane Rowland and Barbara Lyons, "Medicare's Poor, A Background Report on Filling the Gaps in Medical Coverage for Low-Income Elderly Americans" (Paper prepared for the Commonwealth Fund Commission on Elderly People Living Alone, Johns Hopkins University, School of Hygiene and Public Health, 1988), p. 9.
11. Task Force on Long-Term Health Care Policies, *Report to Congress and the Secretary, Department of Health and Human Services*, September 1987, pp. 72–74.
12. Dona DeSanctis, "Private Options in Long-Term Care," *Business and Health* (June 1988), p. 12.
13. See Pamela Doty, "Family Care of the Elderly: The Role of Public Policy," *Milbank Memorial Fund Quarterly*, vol. 64, no. 1 (1986), pp. 34–75.
14. Lynn Paringer, "The Forgotten Costs of Informal Long-Term Care," Urban Institute Working Paper, No. 1466–28, Washington, D.C., 1984.
15. Deborah J. Chollet and Robert B. Friedland, "Employer Financing of Long-Term Care," Employee Benefit Research Institute, 1987, pp. 13–14.
16. Harris and Associates, "Problems Facing Elderly Americans Living Alone," Nationwide Survey Prepared for the Commonwealth Fund Commission on Elderly People Living Alone, New York, 1986.
17. Glenn Collins, "Many in Work Force Care for Elderly Kin," *New York Times*, January 6, 1986.
18. Arthur Lifson, "Long-Term Care: An Insurer's Perspective," in *Long-Term Care Financing and Delivery Systems: Exploring Some Alternatives* (Washington, D.C., 1984), p. 35.
19. Doty, "Family Care of the Elderly."

20. See Mark R. Meiners, "The Case for Long-Term Care Insurance," *Health Affairs*, vol. 2, no. 2 (Summer 1983), pp. 55–79.

21. Marc A. Cohen et al., "The Financial Capacity of the Elderly to Insure for Long-Term Care," Brandeis University, Health Policy Center, March 1986.

22. See Marc A. Cohen et al., "The Lifetime Risks and Costs of Nursing Home Use among the Elderly," *Medical Care*, vol. 24, no. 12 (December 1986), pp. 1161–72.

23. Cohen et al., "The Financial Capacity of the Elderly to Insure for Long-Term Care."

24. Dona DeSanctis and Lisa Lopez, "Legislators Forge Ahead with Access, Coverage Issues," *Business and Health* (June 1988), p. 14.

11
The Elderly "R" Us

Michael Novak

Thinking about the elderly is unusually self-involving. Each of us has elderly parents or other relatives, whose presence prevents our thinking from becoming too abstract. Moreover (and this point is more securely grasped with every passing year), we will soon enough be elderly ourselves. Thus are we spared the vice of becoming excessively detached from our proposals.

Indeed, we may imagine an immense *self-interest* on the part of the working-age generation in having government assume the major (or better, the total) share of the medical costs of the elderly. Otherwise that younger generation would have to bear these costs itself. Government intervention to meet the medical costs of the elderly members of our families relieves us of great anxieties and, in some cases, potentially ruinous personal costs.

In many other ways our subjective experience is intimately involved in thinking about medical care for the elderly. The medical and technological breakthroughs of the past two decades have wrought their marvels in virtually every family. Through experience, our families have come to know how ordinary and expectable "miracles" have become. Disease and maladies that in earlier generations meant certain death are now—by diagnoses and procedures most of us cannot understand—regularly overcome. Members of our families are outliving medical predicaments that would have brought earlier death to all the long line of their predecessors.

Even in the years since 1960, life expectancy, especially for females, has climbed remarkably. Of the Americans who reached age sixty-five during 1982, males could expect on average to live until age seventy-seven (1994). Females could expect on average to live until age eighty-four (2001). Thus, the number of Americans older than sixty-five has gone up year by year (from 19.5 million in 1970 to 27.4

The author is grateful to Karl Zinsmeister and Scott Walter for helping to assemble the empirical data displayed throughout this paper in connection with the Working Seminar on Family and Welfare, published under the title, *The New Consensus on Family and Welfare* (Washington,D.C.: American Enterprise Institute, 1987).

million in 1986), and the ranks older than seventy-five have increased even more rapidly.[1]

But greater longevity is not the only gain achieved by the elderly during the past two decades. More and more of us are thankful that our parents and other elderly relatives are enjoying greater financial well-being and more energy and activity than most of us remember as being possible for *their* parents. At rates higher than those of the population as a whole, this generation's elderly—the elderly of the years between 1960 and 1985—enjoy a much improved standard of living. In 1959, for example, 35 percent of the elderly fell below the official poverty line. By 1985, this percentage had been cut to less than 13 percent. And, after fully accounting for a panoply of noncash benefits (including Medicare and Medicaid, food stamps, and the like), that rate was cut still further, to just over 3 percent.[2]

In addition, between 1960 and 1980, the real median income of the elderly living without relatives had jumped by 69 percent and of those living in families, by 59 percent. These gains far outstripped those of all other Americans, which were, respectively, 41 percent for those living alone and 25 percent for those in families. Usually, the most prosperous age group (aged forty-five to fifty-four) improves its position at higher rates than others. During this twenty-year interval, however, the elderly in families improved their real median income by a significantly higher percentage than their younger counterparts: 59 to 49 percent. During the 1980s, moreover, the elderly in all five income brackets (quintiles) gained more in real income than did the nonelderly.[3]

Perhaps the best indicator of how well the elderly have been doing financially is shown in their preference for maintaining independent households. In 1960, 80 percent of Americans over sixty-five did so, and 58 percent of those over seventy-five. By 1984, these percentages had grown to 91 percent and 86 percent.[4] This preference for independent living is remarkable when we consider that it lowers the total resources available to the elderly, compared with the resources available to those who share a household with other family members. Their preference for independent living, in other words, suggests confidence in their financial security.

In addition, three quarters of the elderly owned their own homes in 1985; and the vast majority of these (84 percent) owned their homes outright. As is well known, the value of real estate appreciated substantially between 1960 and 1985. This fact probably helps to explain why more than 71 percent of the elderly in 1984 showed a net worth that exceeded $25,000. Indeed, the *median* net worth of all the elderly was $60,266.[5] And nearly 25 percent of the elderly whose incomes fell *below* the official poverty line in 1985 had at least $50,000 in home equity.[6]

A lower rate of participation in the labor force reflects a similar improvement. (This is an improvement, at least, insofar as it results in an easier life for the elderly—if not for the solvency of the retirement system.) In 1950, nearly 50 percent of elderly males were in the labor force; by 1985, this percentage had tumbled to 16 percent. Indeed, by 1985, fewer than half the men aged sixty-two to sixty-four were still in the labor force. And nearly two-thirds of those who retired early did so "by choice," only one quarter because of "physical disability."[7]

The elderly, then, enjoy many newfound capacities—to retire from the labor force, to maintain their own independent households, to maintain a significant net worth, and to enjoy the greater longevity made possible by contemporary medical care. Yet it is not only in these that, on average, the situation of the elderly in our families has improved so markedly. Clearly enough, the elderly are more mobile in their choice of residence. They remain remarkably active in many associations, private and public, formal and informal. They travel for pleasure a great deal more frequently and more comfortably. And the far-flung lives of their children and grandchildren carry them to regions of the United States (and the world) that, during the 1930s, they never imagined they would experience. Finally—although this last point is necessarily impressionistic—if we set photographs of our parents at various ages alongside photographs of their parents at a comparable age, ours appear to be at least a decade younger.

In a society as moralistic as ours, it is quite normal to blame ourselves for our many failures. Nonetheless, the condition of the current generation of the elderly represents a quiet triumph of the modern effort to make life better. Most of our elderly relatives never imagined fifty years ago that they would now be living at their current levels of health and energy, and living as well. We hear from them, rather often, words of thankfulness—and surprise.

Most of the elderly live in families (almost always, as we have seen, independently of their children). This was true of 19 million of the 27 million elderly in 1985. Still, this leaves 8.1 million of the elderly living alone. To live alone is not, of course, an unmixed blessing. On the one hand, it sometimes indicates not only a desire but a capacity to live alone. On the other, it has costs, anxieties, and sorrows—and, sometimes, real deprivations and vulnerabilities. By far, most of the elderly who live alone, as their comparatively higher longevity would suggest, are women.

Of the 3.2 million elderly who do need outside help to live alone, about 60 percent say they receive all the help they need, and another 33 percent, *some* of that help. This last figure means that about 1 million of the elderly are in some considerable need. Some scores of thousands of others (the remaining 7 percent) appear to be without the help they need.

Of the elderly who receive all the help they need to live alone (1.9 million), 71 percent receive most of this care from relatives. Another 21 percent receive a mixture of unpaid and paid care (including, for example, services that relatives are not able to provide). Only 8 percent rely exclusively on paid care.[8]

It is worrisome that there are the 1.3 million elderly who live alone and do need care but who receive only some or none of that care. The law makes such persons eligible for benefits. Even so, there is often a considerable gap between what is available and the wide variety of needs among the individuals for whom it is intended, some of whom need assistance but do not or cannot avail themselves of it. In our own vast, continental society, marked by so much mobility that many persons may find themselves separated from their families and longtime friends, there will always need to be extensive efforts, private and public, to seek out those in need and unable by themselves to find assistance. This may be particularly true of elderly persons who are infirm, shut-in, inaccessible, or non-English-speaking. In virtually every urban and rural area, through special vigilance the younger community may find significant numbers of the elderly whose needs, if undiscovered, go unmet. The availability of public or private aid must certainly be matched with concerted outreach.

Much of the success of governmental and private attempts to alleviate the conditions of the elderly since the 1930s, and especially since the 1960s, is probably due to the politics of universality. In most programs (for example, social security), every citizen was made eligible for assistance, in the hope that political support would be equally universal. On the whole, care has been taken to present these programs as consistent both with personal contributions made and with due respect for the value of self-reliance.

The American conscience has been less amenable to appeals to "solidarity," "redistribution," or "equality" than have citizens of Sweden and other advanced capitalist societies. We Americans do not like the idea of making one another automatically dependent upon the state. To us, the idea of social benefits without commensurate personal obligations is somehow abhorrent. Thus, most Americans seem to believe that they have *earned* their social security benefits, just as if they had paid into a private pension plan, the returns of which accrued to them as from an investment fund. This holds even though social security has never actually been funded in the way private pension funds are.

In the same frame of mind, we Americans have so far refused to accept the concept of universal national health insurance on the model of other Western nations such as Sweden, the United Kingdom, and Canada. The fear of massive bureaucratic control over services, practices, and fees appears to be deeper among us than among other peoples.

We may speculate about why this is so. The American experience is rooted in settling a large continent, building a new society, and founding scores of thousands of new communities. We have therefore come to value highly the personal qualities of those who made significant social contributions by dint of their own independent imagination and resolve. Perhaps Americans early and consistently learned to single out doers from shirkers. Clearly, we have never come to believe that human beings are more or less helpless before fate. For generations, Americans have faced so many challenges in the enterprises of surviving, of surmounting odds, and of creating new communities that we could not, and did not, rank either security or egalitarianism high on our tablets of basic values. These did not meet our experience of life.

By contrast, in cultures in which a high proportion of life's chances are fixed at birth, or decided by outside forces, it may make sense to demand equal outcomes for all and certain basic securities. If individuals cannot make their own chances, at least they ought to receive a basic, just, and secure allowance of necessities. Faced with life's hazards, Americans have never been passive in this fashion. We have more highly valued opportunity, risk, daring, and a lighter yoke of regulation. To value a person, Americans have learned, is to value that person's capacity for unusual, even unique, accomplishments. Thus Americans have a profound instinct for the sort of justice that respects *in*equalities, *un*equal outcomes, and individualized deserts. In the circumstances of other nations, in which individuality is neither permitted nor expected to emerge, this American habit of mind (which Americans have taken to be a higher standard of consciousness) seems quite unrealistic. In such foreign circumstances, individual effort and desert being irrelevant, the most justice can aim at is equal shares of basic necessities.

Suppose that the following offer were made to citizens of various cultures: *A new benefit will be made available to all, but only in proportion to individual performance. Everyone will receive more but, according to accomplishment, some will receive still more than others.* I suspect that, in some cultures, citizens would overwhelmingly reject such a scheme,

181

preferring a system in which everyone receives less but all receive the same, according to a strict equality of outcomes. By contrast, most Americans would not only accept this proposal and find it obviously just, but would also (a) hold that it represents a *higher* form of justice and (b) regard the strictly egalitarian impulse as a base and deplorable form of envy (cutting off one's nose to spite one's face).

However this may be, a comparative examination of systems of health care in various nations shows that Americans *have* made quite different political choices from those made by Swedes, Germans, French, British, Canadians, and others (see the chapter by Allen Schick). Americans rather fiercely resist a form of egalitarianism that others have so far found acceptable.

At the same time, Americans have put in place substantial programs designed specifically for those in need, according to means tests. They accept appeals to their compassion; they reject appeals to an egalitarian principle. Even with respect to social security, the principle of universality was never confused with the egalitarian principle. Where differential contributions were made, differential outcomes were also promised. Even if these differences were more symbolic than real (nearly all recipients of social security today receive far more than they actually contributed), they protect for public opinion an important principle.

With regard to health care, however, a meritocratic analysis is difficult to justify. Those who take better care of themselves, other things being equal, are likely to need health care *less*. Preventive care and sound habits can contribute to long and healthful living. But even taking that into account, the hazards of life—from accidents to stress, from a genetic weakness to environmental circumstances—are not distributed according to human merit. Regarding our health needs, we are more in the hands of the fates than we are with respect to the outcomes of our voluntary actions. Thus, medical care is not the same as other market goods, even though the disciplines of the market may make positive contributions to health care. The market, for example, encourages services and inventions that mere bureaucratic control is not likely to inspire. It also tends to draw the highest possible talent to the field. Still, the meritocratic principle here appears to play a somewhat paradoxical role. The worse care people take of themselves and the more intemperate their habits, the more likely they are to need health care—and the more resources they are likely to use.

So if health care is regarded as a benefit, it is not exactly conferred as a reward. Nor is a need for health care ordinarily regarded as a blessing. When we do have the need, though, it is surely a blessing to have the care available. And the poor typically need health care more often, and at greater cumulative cost, than do the well-off.

In a word, in most aspects of our lives we Americans regard responsible personal behavior as meritorious and expect it to enjoy greater rewards than less responsible behavior. But this calculus does not fit well with respect to health care. The reward for responsible care of one's own health is not to *need* health care, unless due to causes beyond one's own control. Such causes occur frequently enough to inspire 85 percent of the American public to seek, and to find, health insurance.

The problem remains, however, that a substantial 15 percent, some 30 million persons, do not have medical insurance. In many other cultures, considerations of security and egalitarianism would lead naturally either to universal insurance or to universal direct provision of health care administered by the state. By contrast—and in deference to American historical experience and learned scales of values—it would seem politically wise to try to extend coverage to these uninsured citizens through some device that requires personal contributions, except in cases of total incapacity to pay. Compassion is highly regarded, whereas free ridership is not.

Finally, while it is true that the elderly "R" us, perhaps most of the more affluent among us would agree that the prognosis for the elderly of our generation is quite favorable. We in our turn will probably not need all the benefits allotted by government with the needs of an earlier generation in mind. Perhaps some universally acceptable formula can be devised whereby the more affluent would accept some downward revision of the benefits currently due us, but probably not needed by us, in favor of applying government resources to younger cohorts plainly in greater need. The most acceptable formula would probably have to include contingency clauses, *in case* some among us came to be needier than it now appears.

Since *we* will be the elderly of the not-so-distant future, perhaps it is time that we try to measure our probable needs with a cold eye, asking ourselves the most difficult of all political questions: Are there really some scheduled benefits from government that we are in a position to forgo, so that government might transfer some additional measure of resources to the generations to which our children, and their children, belong?

It is as if we were to say to ourselves: Ask not what our children can do for us, but what we can do for our children.

Notes

1. Calculated from U.S. Department of Commerce, Bureau of the Census, Series P-60, no. 154, *Money Income and Poverty Statistics of Families and Persons in the United States: 1985 (Advance Data from the March 1986 Current Population Survey)* (Washington, D.C., 1986), table 16.

2. Ibid.; and U.S. Department of Commerce, Bureau of the Census, Technical Paper 53, *Estimates of Poverty including the Value of Noncash Benefits: 1985* (Washington, D.C., 1986), table 1.

3. See Bruce Jacobs, "The Elderly: How Do They Fare?" (Paper presented at the Working Seminar on the Family and American Welfare Policy, Washington, D.C., October 11, 1986; revised, January 1987), p. 6, mimeo. Jacobs derived his figures from Susan Grad, "Incomes of the Aged and Nonaged, 1950–82," *Social Security Bulletin* no. 47 (June 1984).

4. Ibid., p. 11, table 1.

5. U.S. Department of Commerce, Bureau of the Census, Series P-70, no. 7, *Household Wealth and Asset Ownership: 1984* (Washington, D.C., 1985), p. 18.

6. Jacobs, "The Elderly," p. 30.

7. Ibid., p. 12, citing U.S. Senate Special Committee on Aging, *Developments in Aging: 1985*, Report 99–242, vol. 3 (Washington, D.C., 1985), pp. 56–57, 61.

8. Spencer Rich, "Daily Needs Not Met for Many Elderly," *Washington Post*, January 17, 1987.

Index

About the Editors

MARION EIN LEWIN is a senior staff officer at the Institute of Medicine of the National Academy of Sciences. Before that she was director of the Center for Health Policy Research at the American Enterprise Institute. From 1978 to 1983 she served as associate director of the National Health Policy Forum, a nonpartisan educational program for high-level federal, state, and private sector specialists in health affairs. She is coeditor of *The Economics and Ethics of Long-Term Care and Disability* (1988), *Charting the Future of Health Care: Policy, Politics, and Public Health* (1987), and *From Research into Policy: Improving the Link for Health Services* (1986) and editor of *The Health Policy Agenda: Some Critical Questions* (1985), all published by AEI.

SEAN SULLIVAN is vice president of New Directions for Policy, a research and policy analysis firm in Washington, D.C. He was a senior policy analyst at AEI. He is coauthor of *Providing Mental Health Benefits: Alternatives for Employers* (1987), *Buying Smart: Business Strategies for Managing Health Care Costs* (1986), *Managing Health Care Costs: Private Sector Innovation* (1984), and *Passing the Health Care Buck: Who Pays the Hidden Cost?* and coeditor of *The Economics and Ethics of Long-Term Care and Disability* (1988) and *Restructuring Medicaid: A Survey of State and Local Initiatives*, all published by AEI.

A Note on the Book
This book was edited by Trudy Kaplan,
Dana Lane, and Janet Schilling of the
publications staff of the American Enterprise Institute.
The index was prepared by Evanthia Speliotis.
The text was set in Palatino, a typeface designed by Hermann Zapf.
Coghill Composition Company, of Richmond, Virginia,
set the type, and Edwards Brothers Incorporated,
of Ann Arbor, Michigan, printed and bound the book,
using permanent acid-free paper.